Robert S. Woodbury

EPM
Publications

This story is true. The opinions expressed
are the author's own. A few names have been
changed to protect the innocent.

Library of Congress Cataloging in Publication Data

Woodbury, Robert Spring, 1935-
    Yen for a yacht.

    1. Charter-parties — St. Lucia. 2. Yachts and
yachting — St. Lucia. I. Title.
HE596.W66   386'.352   79-26932
ISBN 0-914440-30-6

EPM Publications, Inc.
1003 Turkey Run Road
McLean, Virginia 22101
Design by Ice House Graphics

TO MURPHY'S LAW

WITH RESPECT

AND

HUMILITY

MURPHY'S LAW

THE SIX PRINCIPLES

1. In any field of endeavor, anything that can go
wrong, will go wrong.

2. Left to themselves, things always go from bad
to worse.

3. If there is a possibility of several things going
wrong, the one that will go wrong is the one that
will do the most damage.

4. If everything seems to be going well, you have
obviously overlooked something.

5. Calamity seeks the hidden flaw.

6. Mother Nature is a dog.

"Damn you, boat," I screamed, "what do you want from me?"

Hot? God, it was hot in that boat's engine room. Sweat ran into my eyes and stung so badly, I could hardly see. Lying flat on greasy floorboards, sandwiched between a pair of 200-horsepower, hot diesel engines, I had exhausted my mechanical ingenuity and had turned to the court of last resort: swear like hell. The damn bilge pump just wouldn't pump and that was all there was to it. And the waters of the Caribbean were still leaking in from somewhere and filling the bilge at an alarming rate. I was so frustrated my hands were trembling.

"Got problems?" came an unrecognized voice.

A smart ass. Just what I needed. A smart ass. I rolled over so that I could look toward my feet, the general direction of both the voice and the engine room hatch. Fully prepared to hurl any unexpended invective I could muster, I found myself toes to nose with an almost cherubic face connected to a massive and muscular body which seemed to fill the whole hatch-

1

way. He had brown skin and was smiling from ear to ear.

"McDoom's the name," he said. "Peter McDoom."

That was too much. "What the hell is a West Indian doing with a name like McDoom?" I asked, having forgotten my frustration and anger of a moment before.

"My great-grandfather was Scottish," he said simply. "Want some help with that thing?"

At this point, even a total stranger was a better bet than I was, so I expressed my thanks and wormed my way out through the hatch and let him go in. I sat down on the steps leading into the galley, glad to be out of the heat and able to move about, and glad to be out of the engine room where it seemed I had spent all my life. Actually, I had first seen that overheated, greasy sauna only a few months ago.

At that time, I was a public relations executive with a major commercial bank in Boston. Theoretically, I had aspirations; in fact, I was bored to tears. Having once again been given the office and salary of an executive and the responsibilities of a street sweeper, I needed a change.

I had no idea what kind of a change I wanted until my girl friend ran my twin-engine cabin cruiser up on the only shoal ground in Boston's inner harbor. Two new propellers, two new shafts, two new struts and two new rudders later, I was waiting in the outer office of the marina repair shop while they totaled up the bill. It took some time and I occupied myself with the current issue of a boating magazine. My eyes fell on an advertisement and suddenly, the whole world seemed to stop turning . . .

CARIBBEAN CHARTER BUSINESS FOR SALE

57-ft. power cruiser of traditional elegance equipped for permanent live-aboard comfort and engaged in established day charter business. Crew's quarters, modern galley, two private staterooms, two heads, showers, full carpeting, air conditioning. Twin GM 6-71s, generator, radio, dinghy and outboard. Excellent recent survey. Write Carib Cruises, Castries, St. Lucia.

2

After reading the ad, I knew I would have no peace of mind unless I at least wrote for information. The boat would turn out to be a dog, the business a joke and I could forget the whole thing. That is assuming I got any answer at all.

Looking back, I'm not sure just how it happened. Somehow in two months, I traveled to St. Lucia, bought the boat, returned to Boston, negotiated what for me was an astronomical loan at the bank I had been working for (I had a few friends there), told the bank to find a new street sweeper, sold my car, boat and furniture, packed some dirty shirts and some clean socks and said goodby to it all. I was never the same individual after that day.

I first met Beverly Pringle in the morning mail when she replied to my request for more information on the "57-foot power cruiser" she (Carib Cruises) had advertised. Beverly's reply was prompt, businesslike, complete and helpful and I knew right from the start that regardless of what the boat might turn out to be, I had a good broker. And that was one of the main reasons that I decided to go to St. Lucia at once. I flew out the next day.

We touched down in the dead of night at Hewanorra Airfield on the southern tip of St. Lucia. It was there that I began to learn about the West Indies. *Visitor IV* was located at Castries, a port town at the northern end of the Island served by a small airstrip called Vigie. I had been told that I would have to make a connecting flight on Wings Airways from the international airport in the south to the smaller airport up north. I had been impressed. After all, we only had one airport in Boston.

I thought something was a bit strange when I got off the giant 707 and found myself standing on grass rather than the usual acres of macadam, but I strode confidently into the little wooden terminal building and endured the familiar customs and immigration ritual. Then, I searched for an intelligent-looking person to give me directions for my Wings flight.

"Excuse me," I asked a tall, impressive looking customs officer, "could you tell me where the Wings Terminal is?"

3

"Right there," he said, pointing to a dark corner of the small building.

All I could see in the direction where he was pointing was a cluster of tables and chairs which probably served as a kind of restaurant during the day. Obviously, he didn't understand.

"No, I'm sorry. I mean the Wings Airways Terminal. I'm flying up to Castries."

"Man, look me. You see de fella dere he sleepin wid de hat on his face. Dat does be Wings. Terminal, pilot, airplane, anthing Wings you want, he does be it."

I looked harder. Indeed, slouched in one of the chairs, there was someone asleep. I went over to him.

"Excuse me," I said, rather haltingly, "but I'm looking for the Wings Terminal."

"Has the jet left yet?" the hat asked.

I said that it hadn't.

"Well, hold your water. When the jet goes, I'll get the plane out from behind those palm trees over there. If I get it out now, the wash from those jet engines'll blow the damn thing over."

It seemed reasonable.

The jet did take off a few minutes later with a roar that could loosen the fillings in your teeth, and, as the roar abated, it was replaced with the whine and cough of a neat little single-engine plane coming, indeed, out of a clump of palm trees. It rocked to a halt and the pilot got out and beckoned me to come.

"You the only one?" he asked.

There was no one else in sight.

We were in the air in seconds and, after three or four minutes of flying, I was surprised to hear the pilot talking on the plane's loudspeaker.

"Good evening, ladies and gentlemen. On behalf of Captain Parlor and his crew, we would like to welcome you on board Wings Airways Flight One from Hewanorra Airfield to Vigie Airfield. We shall be flying at an altitude of 4,000 feet, flying time 12 minutes. We hope you have a pleasant flight."

I had the distinct feeling that a big city type was being had by a small island pilot. A few months later, Joe Parlor, Jr. and

4

I had a good laugh over that one.

I got up early the next morning and found that St. Lucia Yacht Services was within walking distance from my hotel. It was hot, even at 9:00 in the morning, and I was perspiring after just a few minutes of walking. I was told at the hotel to take a short cut across the Airfield landing strip, but to be sure to look both ways for a plane landing or taking off before crossing. I wondered about St. Lucian Boy Scouts doing a land-office business helping little old ladies across that bit of roadway.

There was a dirt road leading off to the left and next to it a large sign that said "St. Lucia Yacht Services". I kicked up dust with my city shoes as I walked down the road looking for Carib Cruises.

St. Lucia Yacht Services was better known as Ganter's, the name of the long since gone founder of the establishment. Burt Ganter, as best I could tell from very sketchy information, had been a hardworking, hard-drinking ne'er-do-well who had acquired the land and built up a motley little marine repair business. There were no docks, no fuel, no electricity, not much of anything except Burt whom no one seemed to have a good word for and his wife Gracie whom everyone loved as the matriarch of the boating community.

Burt had disappeared a long time ago and later, Gracie had taken in a partner from the United States whose only claim to fame was some badly needed capital. He was a typical absentee owner who occasionally wrote long letters asking why things weren't more profitable and annually returned to St. Lucia to seek the answers to his questions and take a two-week sail on the boat he owned and kept at the marina. He never got his answers and usually went home earlier than anticipated.

His capital was wisely invested in docks, including an excellent fuel dock, as well as in electricity, a large cement building that housed a laundry, a good engine repair shop, equipment lockers for the boats, a chandlery and food store of sorts, a yacht brokerage and charter agency (Carib Cruises) and a marina office. St. Lucia Yacht Services wasn't much but it could hold its head up among its counterparts in neighboring islands and it was to suit me just fine.

When I arrived in St. Lucia, I knew nothing about chartering, nothing about the West Indies or West Indians, nothing about St. Lucia or St. Lucians (I had to look St. Lucia up in the Boston Public Library to find out where it was), nothing about running my own business and nothing about tourism. Without Carib Cruises, Ltd., I wouldn't have made it through the first week. Or the last week for that matter.

Beverly Pringle was all Carib Cruises had. She was the company, except for a so-called board of directors who absorbed losses with typical West Indian grace and occasionally made a nuisance of themselves by showing up at her office at the wrong time. Beverly and her son, Craig, had been living in the West Indies for years, first operating a small hotel with her husband and eventually opening a brokerage and charter business. Her office was tucked between the engine repair shop and the chandlery and food store.

I felt a little stupid as I knocked on her office door for the first time. Here I was, 35 years old, in theory if not in practice an adult, skipping out of a job where I surely belonged, taking an expensive plane trip which I could ill-afford, traveling 2,300 miles to a place I had never heard of with the thought of embarking on a venture about which I knew absolutely nothing. Somehow, I had the feeling that this nice lady would turn out to look something like my mother and would give me the scolding I richly deserved and send me home. I opened the door and walked in.

There she was, sitting behind a desk, a neat, trim, pretty blond in a shocking pink bikini and a flimsy beach cover-up that didn't cover up.

"You must be Mr. Woodbury," she said smilingly.

"How did you know?" I asked.

"I just had a feeling," she said, still smiling.

She was being kind. In the months and years to come, I would see countless prospective buyers come to Beverly's office looking just the way I did that morning—heavy leather street shoes covered with dust, socks that reached to my knees, dark pants that obviously belonged to a matching suit coat, dress shirt fresh out of the laundry open at the neck (I won't wear a tie, I had thought, after all, this is the West Indies) and skin so pasty white that its owner looked like death warmed-over.

Beverly asked me to sit down and the learning process continued for me. I thought I had hundreds of questions but I only asked a few of them because she knew what the questions were, even when I didn't, and volunteered the answers without being asked. Her frankness was disarming and her honesty almost shocking. I began to realize she was a great deal like myself. A spade was clearly a spade and nothing more and if that was going to cost her a sale, then that was the way it would have to be. Of course it wasn't pure altruism; she knew that whoever bought *Visitor IV* would be living right outside her office door and any gilding of the lily would come back to haunt her. Also, ten years in the business world had taught me, if nothing else, to recognize a phony when I saw one and I knew Beverly Pringle was not one.

I remember she asked me at one point why I thought I wanted to buy a boat and go chartering in the West Indies. I wasn't at all sure myself. The best I could do for an answer was to look at my feet and stammer something to the effect that, at age 35, I guessed I had become something of a drop-out.

"What the hell do you think the rest of us here are?" she demanded, and went on to describe what it was like for her to return to her native Montreal, Canada each year to see her parents.

"Every year, Craig and I go back during the off-season, expecting to stay three weeks. We usually come back in two or less. The city, the traffic, the noise, the people . . . my God, the people. I know what living that kind of life does to your outlook and I don't want to be that way. I don't want to think like that, I don't want to live like that."

I was beginning to think I had not only found a friend, but a comrade-in-arms as well. We talked for several hours about St. Lucia, chartering and *Visitor IV*.

7

Suddenly, the office door opened with a bang and a tousled-haired young man of about twelve lurched through the doorway, threw some schoolbooks in an empty corner and slouched in a vacant chair without a word. He was wearing the kind of white shirt and black pants associated with parochial school uniforms; both shirt and pants were covered with the kind of dust and dirt associated with twelve-year-old boys.

"My son, Craig. Craig, this is Mr. Woodbury," said Beverly with mock formality. She suggested to Craig that he go out and get us all some hamburgers and to come back quickly.

Beverly's home was three steps outside her office window and tied up to one of the piers. There was no question that at one time it had been a sailboat because it floated and had a mast, but it floated because of skillful application of cement to strategic places in the bilges and the mast still stood principally because there was very little wind in Vigie Creek. *Maid of Arron,* as she was called, had spent the past seven years of her long life without once moving from the pier.

We ate our hamburgers on board *Maid of Arron* under a canvas canopy which gave us merciful protection from the noonday sun. It was here that I was introduced to the finest alcoholic beverage ever to grace the palate of mankind. I shan't ask you all to rise as I speak the name of Mt. Gay Rum, but you shall have to forgive me if I do so.

Beverly had made arrangements for me to go aboard *Visitor IV* to meet the owner and take a demonstration cruise that afternoon. I had been suspicious of S. Montague Robinson Esq. since I had seen his name under the heading of "owner" on the survey of *Visitor IV,* which Beverly had sent me in her first letter. I had imagined one of those tall, rather scrawny, pasty-faced Britishers with knee-length white socks, white shorts with the pocket linings hanging out underneath the cuffs, and an unironed, well-worn, white bush jacket. I couldn't quite go as far as a monocle and pith helmet but I was sure he would be veddy British and veddy stuffy.

I was right on almost all counts, including the hang-out pockets.

Monty Robinson was not British, however, but rather an

unfortunate kind of mock-British and, in fact, a Canadian. He was the sort of individual who could, with deadly seriousness, refer to his 57-foot motor yacht as "the ship" and the wheelhouse as "the bridge", and require his West Indian crewman to preface any requests made of charterers with "The Captain's compliments, sir, would you . . .". After I bought *Visitor* he used to come around occasionally and offer useless advice on anything from electrical wiring to varnishing, to how to get along with "the locals", as he called them. One day he launched into a lecture on how to manage a West Indian crewman that was eighteenth century colonialism at its best. At one point, he drew his head close to mine and said confidentially, "Of course, one never takes one's meals with them."

In any case, Beverly introduced us and then had the good sense to leave. We were to get under way at once and the engines were running when we came aboard. Robinson seemed a nervous wreck. He was covered with sweat and his bush jacket was soaked. His handshake was wet and clammy and, fortunately, brief.

Some months later I discovered, from a friend I had made at Ganter's, that the *Visitor*'s former owner was so unnerved every time he took "the ship" to sea that he was frequently sick to his stomach before he could go up to the wheelhouse and start the engines.

The demonstration cruise was uneventful except that the autopilot power supply went up in smoke, a warning of things to come with regard to *Visitor*'s electrical system.

Visitor IV was just what I had wanted. She was a classy old lady and she was a mess. Built in 1941, at Annapolis Yacht Yard (just before it was purchased by John Trumpy), and designed by Nelson and Almen, *Visitor* was one of the last of a dying breed. She had the bow of a destroyer, the bilge and keel of a trawler and a hard chine in the stern of a planing hull. Weighing 41 tons, she was supposed to have a top speed of 16 knots. I never had the heart to push her hard enough to find out if that were true , but I think she might have been capable of it in her youth.

Yet some of her beauty and class still shone through the

years of neglect. Her salon was paneled in a lovely dark teak, just visible through too many layers of varnish. It had a built-in secretary with real leaded glass windows in the cabinet doors. There was a drop-leaf mahogany dining table that would have brought tears to the eyes of an antique collector. But the floor was covered with institutional green indoor-outdoor carpeting that clearly had been out more than in. The sofa had layers of coverings, including, from inside out: first, the original cracked and torn, white plastic upholstery; next, a faded and stained, pink fitted slipcover; then, an unfitted, flower print throw cover; and last, but by no means least, a nondescript bedspread. Lovely.

Visitor did have two very pleasant double staterooms, one with a full double bed which was an unheard-of luxury on a yacht of her vintage. The main head had an electric flush toilet which never once failed to function in the three years to come, and, the most incredible thing on the whole boat, a full size, stainless steel bathtub.

In the stern, she had a covered cockpit which was big enough for eight to ten people to congregate and a fold-down table which was to support many a moonlit, Caribbean evening dinner . . . candles, wine, the whole bit.

The galley was just about perfect except for an antiquated propane gas hot water heater which was mounted right in the middle of the only available counter space. The genius who installed it had forgotten to include an outside vent, so that while the temperature in that little galley hovered around the 100-degree mark, the fumes dulled your senses to the point where you hardly cared. That beast was one of the first things to go and was replaced by an under-the-counter electric job.

The crew's quarters of every small yacht is its least commendable feature and *Visitor* was no exception: two very uncomfortable vee bunks and a head and shower that had to be completely replaced in the course of time.

My real pride and joy on the old girl was the wheelhouse. She had a completely separate, raised wheelhouse with a clear view of the whole boat including the stern. There was a proper chart table and a long, full width upholstered seat

10

across the back. The woodwork had so many layers of varnish that it appeared to be black and neither grain nor bungs were visible. When the time came to set the crewman to work stripping it, I was delighted to find the whole thing was solid mahogany.

The engine room was something else again. Chaos is perhaps too strong a word but it will do. Tucked into every nook and cranny in that engine room was the damnedest collection of pumps and associated piping and wiring that I had ever seen . . . all of it inaccessible, incomprehensible and irresponsible. There seemed to be wires of every size, color and shape going in every direction, a good many of them terminating at their own end rather than at some particular electrical device for which they might have been installed. In short, their purposes had long been lost to history. There were equally as many assorted bits of piping, hoses and valves which seemed to serve no purpose. Frankly, I felt sure the whole thing could go up in smoke at any moment.

The two engines seemed my only hope of survival at sea. They were clean, well-painted, started quickly and ran smoothly. I had no real idea of their history or even their age, but I had been told by a good friend, who had a lifelong experience with them, that a General Motors 6—71 would run forever. I guess he was right because although I was to work my heart out over virtually every other piece of machinery on that boat in the years to come, the only thing I did to the engines was to change an occasional water pump and an exhaust manifold. They never missed a beat in three years.

Out on deck, thinks looked a little better. The decks, while worn, were teak with that nice weathered gray color that teak deck lovers appreciate so much. All of the superstructure was solid mahogany. In fact, I never found a piece of plywood in the hull or superstructure except what had obviously been added after the boat had left her builders. *Visitor* was all business when it came to ground tackle (anchoring equipment). She had three anchors, 250 feet of 3/4-inch nylon line, 250 feet of anchor chain and an electric windlass with rope capstan and chain gypsy. That windlass was to give me some of

11

my worst hours on *Visitor.*

The old girl desperately needed a coat of paint and the little bit of brightwork that had survived the onslaught of previous owners' paintbrushes also needed work. But none of it was so bad that it would require that backbreaking take-it-down-to-the-wood process. There was hope that she could be made to look like the lady she once was, and fairly quickly. Putting her confused insides to rights was another thing.

At this point, if not before, anyone with even basic boating sense would wonder why in hell I bought *Visitor IV.* Let me tell you, she was just what I wanted. First and foremost, she was somewhat established in a moneymaking business. I couldn't afford a boat like this unless it could pay its way. In spite of Robinson's shortcomings, both as a yachtsman and a human being, none of them had come through to a single charterer and *Visitor* had a surprisingly good reputation as a day charter boat. Very few, if any, guests returned to their hotel with anything but rave notices for their day on *Visitor IV.* This kept the hotel managers happy and they continued to recommend the boat.

Secondly, she was big and comfortable enough to live aboard. Not only was that something I wanted to do anyway, it also cut down on the overhead tremendously.

Thirdly, and most importantly for me personally, *Visitor* was a mess. You see, I was born a Mr. Fix-it. I can fix most anything and I get more satisfaction out of doing so than out of anything else in life. A properly installed, properly maintained and properly functioning anything is a joy to me and it only makes me happier if I did it.

I was raised, on the other hand, in an environment which espoused the method of going to college and wearing a white shirt and tie so you can afford to have someone else fix it. I tried it. I tried it for more than ten years and it was interesting for a while. The business world seemed to operate just as I had been told it did: do a good job, become recognized as hardworking and talented, and you will be rewarded. I was. I was promoted from recruit clerk to junior clerk to clerk to lieutenant clerk and finally to senior clerk. But the theory held that one should be able to go right to the top. I had often wondered about that because there obviously wasn't much room at the top, and there were a lot of us trying to get there.

After ten years, I thought I had better stop, take a long look back and make an assessment of where I was. Something didn't seem to be right: I wasn't getting to the top. In fact, I wasn't sure I wanted to be there. The price seemed too high. I had come to know a lot of those who were at or near the top and it seemed to me that beyond a certain point, the way was paved with con jobs, yessir, that's a great idea, the public be damned, the customer be damned, outright fraud and hooray for me and the hell with you. Clearly, I was at that point and it was time to get with it or get out. I felt if I couldn't succeed in the business world by doing things the right way, then I had best find another world to succeed in. If it meant taking off the white shirt and tie and getting my hands dirty, that was all right because I really enjoyed doing that more anyway.

And so I bought the Motor Yacht *Visitor IV*, sold everything I owned and flew back to St. Lucia, walked once again across the landing strip, down the dirt road to Ganter's and aboard my new floating home. That night I slept like a baby.

There was so much to be done on the boat that I thought I would get to know the Island a bit first. The heat seemed too intense for work because there was an acclimation process that we who came from northern climates had to go through before we could hope to feel comfortable.

St. Lucia was one of the so-called Windward Islands, part of a volcanic chain running from Florida to South America. Only 13 degrees north of the equator, it was 27 miles long in a north-south direction and 14 miles wide. Its 238 square miles varied from lush green mountains in the north and central regions to quite parched flat land in the south.

Mt. Gimie was St. Lucia's highest peak at 3,145 feet, but its most famous landmarks were the twin peaks on the east coast that rose straight up from the ocean floor to 2,619 and 2,461 feet. Called the Gros and Petit Piton, they have been a mariner's landfall for centuries.

Their saddle dropped off into the most beautiful bay in the West Indies. Coconut palm trees came down to the water's edge and a pastoral assortment of goats, pigs and chickens roamed among them. Thatched roof huts sheltered a few fishing canoes and almost always a busy group of fishermen were coming or going. Their wives and children whiled away idyllic days playing under the palm trees or harvesting coconuts for St. Lucia's thriving copra industry. The water was crystal clear and a snorkeler's paradise. Anse des Pitons, as the bay was called, could also be a yacht captain's headache: the anchoring was poor and the two pitons created a canyon effect. It could become pure unannounced hell when, for no apparent reason, hurricane force winds came out of nowhere within minutes.

It was the British who made the first attempts to settle St. Lucia in 1605 and later in 1638, but it was discovered by shipwrecked seamen from a French vessel in 1502. After that, the island changed hands 14 times by the way of some of the bloodiest battles ever fought between the British and French. No doubt Peter McDoom's great-grandfather came with the British forces. Seagoing battles were launched from the nearby French island of Martinique and British Barbados. It was from tiny Pigeon Island off the north shore of St. Lucia that Admiral Rodney destroyed the French fleet in one of the decisive naval engagements of European history.

Finally, the Treaty of Paris in 1814 ceded St. Lucia to Britain and there was peace from then on. On March 1, 1967, St. Lucia became a member of the West Indies Associated States with full control over her internal affairs. Britain was responsible only for her defense and foreign affairs. By 1970, there were more than 120,000 St. Lucians and, while English was the official language, most spoke a unique patois that was a combination of French and Swahili.

The capital was the port city of Castries and Vigie Creek, where St. Lucia Yacht Services was located, lay in the north corner of the Harbor. Fortunately, Castries was large enough to have a good supply of the day-to-day needs of a yacht such

as marine paint, sandpaper, electrical and plumbing hardware and so on.

One of life's little pleasures during my time in St. Lucia was
to hop into my dinghy, whip up the Sea Gull outboard and
buzz out into Castries Harbor and across to the town. There
was a spot among the docks where dinghys could tie up and a
little brown friend named Charlie was always there to keep an
eye on my craft for "small change" while I shopped for a can
of paint or a piece of pipe. The harbor even had a slipway
which could handle my 41-ton *Visitor IV,* although this was
destroyed later as part of a massive redesigning and dredging
of the harbor.

From Castries, there was a new road which took you the six
or seven miles to the very northern tip of the island in minutes. The road to the south was a winding, climbing, falling,
narrow, terror-filled roller coaster which would clock 57 miles
in two hours to reach the southern tip—a distance of about 20
miles as the crow flew. Drive it once and you would wish you
were that crow.

I got my first taste of boating many years ago when I was a junior in high school. At the beginning of summer vacation, I hadn't lined up a job and I was restless. I went over to talk with my best friend in those days, Angus Kennedy. Angus and I had known each other since we had been in summer camps when we were knee-high to the proverbial grasshopper. We had sneaked our first cigarettes together out in back of the schoolhouse and used to go on double dates to the drive-in. We were big time in those days.

But the cigarettes and the double dating had worn a little thin that summer and we wanted to find something really exciting to do. We had been kicking around ideas for weeks when Angus got a lead.

"What do ya say we take a boat trip?" he asked tentatively.

"OK," I said. "Where you going to get the boat?" thinking that would end the idea at once. I knew Angus' dad had owned a lovely old 30-foot Balsa Jonesport, but he had taken it to the Virgin Islands years ago to start a boating business.

The business had failed and the boat had stayed there in other hands.

"I got a boat," he replied. "Down in back of the house. You remember that 11-foot aluminum job we always had. Well, there's a 10-horse Johnson that goes with it and I think it still works."

"Christ, Gus. Where the hell we gonna go in an 11-foot boat with a 10-horse Johnson?" I asked.

"Listen, with decent weather, you can go anywhere with an 11-foot boat. It isn't the size of the boat, it's the size of the waves and if it gets rough, you just head for shore. You listen to weather forecasts and keep an eye on the sky. And you stay close to shore and follow the chart."

I listened to him for some time. Angus had a little boating experience with his Dad and I could only assume he knew what he was talking about. The more we talked, the more, in my naive way, I thought we knew what we were talking about. Having convinced ourselves that the idea was a good one, we set about planning where to go. We thought that it would be fun to take everything we would need for the trip with us, except gasoline for the outboard. We would have to put into port for that. Otherwise, we wanted to be self-sufficient for the duration of the trip.

We made plans to camp out overnight on shore and, after a lot of calculation and discarded possibilities, we charted a trip from Boston Harbor to Providence, Rhode Island of about 120 miles by water. It is indicative of the coast we planned to travel past to note that such a trip would be about 45 miles by land. We planned to be gone for three nights and a total of four days under way.

I was commissioned chief engineer and Angus navigator. We figured we didn't need a captain and besides there wasn't room for one anyway. We were both our purchasing agents and worked hard to find what we would need at the lowest cost. Space was at a premium as well and that played a big role in selection of goods. Some things simply had to be included such as our two sleeping bags, the pup tent Angus owned, the two fuel tanks, a jerry can of water and a jerry can of gasoline for emergency use only.

We knew we were going to get wet if the seas got the least bit rambunctious, so we needed watertight containers for our food and other things which could be damaged by water. Large surplus ammunition cans were perfect and we squandered $10.00 each for two of them, one of our best investments.

When everything was assembled at Angus' house, we dragged the boat out from under the porch, set it upright on the lawn and conducted a dry-run loading to see if everything would fit in and still leave room for the navigator and engineer. It did. Just. That evening, we plotted all the courses on the charts that we expected to need. There would be no parallel rule wizardry aboard our little cockleshell once we were at sea. It was going to be "one hand for the ship and one for your life" and we knew it.

I had done a tune-up on the somewhat antiquated Johnson outboard motor and stocked a reasonable supply of spare parts and tools. We had two life preservers, railroad flares, a hand bilge pump, binoculars, a change of clothes, foul weather gear, an incredibly inexpensive compass for which we never had the chance to make a deviation table or compensate, an anchor and line, a flashlight and matches in a special waterproof case. We put most of the food in the one ammo case and the safety and navigation equipment and clothes in the other.

At last the big day arrived. Angus' dad was in the interior decorating business and had a pickup truck in which we could load everything to take to Boston Harbor for the launching. The aluminum boat was relatively light and, with Mr. Kennedy's help, we got it into and out of the truck easily. On arrival at our launching site, we unloaded everything and spread it out on the dock. Then each item was carefully loaded aboard and secured in place. We knew we didn't want anything adrift while under way. By the time the motor was in place, the boat was somewhat down on her normal water line. When we both got in, Angus' father looked at the whole thing

19

with noticeable concern. We had about 12 to 15 inches of free-board but the boat had built-in flotation compartments and, in a real emergency, we could jettison everything.

We had put a lot of planning into it and, with everything neatly packed into its proper place, we thought it looked pretty good. Looking back on it, I think we were too young to be suitably afraid.

We returned to the truck to listen for the latest weather forecast on its radio. In those days, all we could get on the AM radio was the 60-second special squashed in after the news and it never had much to do with sea and wind conditions. But it was all there was and it talked about a bright, sunny day with temperatures in the 80s. We were ready.

We said good-by to Mr. Kennedy and promised to call him when we got to Plymouth, our first stop. As engineer, I fired up the outboard and we were off.

The wind was cool out in the Harbor and I pulled the hood of my sweatshirt over my head. The boat splashed a little spray over the bow and I tasted salt water on my lips. I turned and looked at Angus and smiled.

"By God, we made it," I said gleefully.

"Made it is right," said Angus. He was dressed much the same as I was, dungarees, hooded sweatshirt over a light woolen shirt and sneakers with heavy socks. He had a big ten-gallon hat he had bought as a souvenir on a trip to Texas long ago. Now it was just the thing to shade his eyes from the early morning sun. Angus was scanning the water for his first channel marker.

"Should be a nun buoy on our right," he called out. "We'll take our first bearing from that."

"Oh my God!" Angus exclaimed. The little boat was just passing a headland which formed Point Allerton and Angus was looking at a neat white building on some high ground on the point.

"What's wrong?" I asked.

"Look," said Angus pointing at the building. "Small craft warnings."

On a mast on the top of the building was a red pennant-shaped flag flapping in the brisk morning air.

"Is that the Coast Guard Station?" I asked.

"Yah."

"What'll we do?"

"Let's go on out and see how bad it is. They put that thing up at the drop of a hat. It might not be too bad."

I kept the bow of the boat headed straight out the channel. I could see flecks of white out on the water and knew it would be choppy. The boat began to pitch a little as the bow rose up and down on the light swells just outside the Harbor. Angus folded the chart once more and put it under his shirt. He didn't want it to get wet.

There was a good breeze and the sea was far from calm but up to now neither of us had been concerned. Suddenly the bow dipped alarmingly and I reached for the lines holding the ammunition cans in place. A fine sheet of water sprayed back on the two of us as the bow drove through an oncoming wave.

"Jesus," exclaimed Angus, wiping water from his face.

"It's getting a little rough."

"Yah, I know," I said as I slowed the motor. "Why don't you dig out the foul weather gear, Gus?"

He unlocked the cover of one of the waterproof ammunition cans and took out two plastic rain parkas and gave one to me.

I felt the boat lurching under me and began to wonder if this had been such a good idea after all. The waves were getting bigger as we went farther and farther out. I looked back to shore and realized I could no longer see the little red flag on top of the Coast Guard station. It was too far away.

"Jesus, Angus, do you think this is OK? I mean isn't it getting kinda rough?"

"It's not bad. The boat's riding the waves good. As long as the bow doesn't dip down too far we're OK. Besides it should be better when we change course."

Each time the boat crested the top of a wave, Angus scanned the ocean for a channel marker.

"There's bell three," he said.

"Good," said I, who had never relaxed my grip on the securing line since the first big wave. "I hope that will be a more peaceful course."

The new course was smoother after all and Angus offered to take a turn at the motor. Several hours of steady cruising passed uneventfully with the little boat bobbing along in the bright sunshine, heading south toward the Cape Cod Canal. The earlier excitement had subsided and suddenly we realized we were very hungry.

"Hey, how about some chow?" I asked.

"Sure, why not?" said Angus. He unlatched one of the ammo cans and withdrew a loaf of bread, a jar of mayonnaise and a can of sardines. After some juggling, he produced two very large and very messy sardine sandwiches. These were quickly consumed and washed down with a can each of Coke.

It was early in the afternoon when Angus announced Plymouth Harbor was in sight. By three o'clock we had followed Plymouth's winding channel and were coming alongside the fishing pier. It was low tide and, when the boat had been tied to a piling, we had to climb up a ladder to reach the top of the pier. I was first up the ladder. As I climbed over the edge of the pier I suddenly felt a wave of nausea.

"My God, I think I'm land sick, Gus," I called down. "Man, what a weird feeling! I think if I stand up, I'll fall down," I said half seriously.

Angus' head appeared at the top of the ladder. He was carrying one of the gasoline cans, empty from the day's cruising.

"I see what you mean," exclaimed Angus. The two of us sat there on the pier laughing over the strange feeling. We were joined by two men who had been packing ice and fish from a trawler into wooden crates.

"Howdy," said one of them peering over the edge at the boat below. "Where you guys headed?" he asked, looking at the gas tanks and camping equipment.

"Providence, Rhode Island," Angus volunteered.

"Only Providence you'll get to in that boat isn't in Rhode Island," the fishermen said.

"Whadaya mean?" Angus exclaimed. "We got this far from Boston and you should have see it out there."

"Boston? Hey, Charlie, look at this," the fisherman said

calling to another man still packing ice and fish. By now, five or six men had come to see the adventurers and their boat. Gus and I got up and headed toward the gas pumps at the end of the pier.

"Think they'd never seen a boat before, wouldn't you?" said Angus with a smile.

"Ya, how about that?"

It wasn't long before we had loaded up with gas and, after phoning Angus' father to let him know all was well, were off again. Angus thought that a good camp site could be found on the peninsula which formed the Harbor. We took the boat up and down the leeward side looking for a suitable place. Eventually we headed for shore and beached the boat. Soon, we had a driftwood fire going. Canned stew never tasted so good to me. It was just dusk by the time the little tent was set up with the two sleeping bags inside.

When we awoke, the damp cold of early morning was everywhere and my first thought was to get a fire going. The tent, the sleeping bag, shoes, everything I touched was wet with dew.

By the time we had eaten breakfast, packed the boat and were under way, the sun was well above the horizon. The water was as flat as glass and I felt guilty disturbing its placidness with the bow of the boat. Our craft seemed to be skimming along the top of the water and it was strange not to be bucking the waves.

"It's so calm, it's dull," I said.

"It sure is," replied Angus. "Why don't you open it up and we can make a little time? We want to hit the Cape Cod Canal by noon or we'll be bucking the tide."

I twisted the motor's steering handle and the motor picked up. We kept up speed for several hours, slowing only to change positions to take turns steering the motor. The bright sun glistened on the water and we had to squint even with sunglasses. I was glad I had thought to bring a hat with me, but I envied Angus' big Texas hat and the shade it offered. It was eleven o'clock when we found the first marker for the Canal. Angus offered to take the boat through for he had experience that might be needed. As the boat entered the Canal, we felt it accelerate under the power of the tide.

"It's a good thing the tide's with us," I called out. "We'd never make it otherwise."

We continued on through the Canal out into Buzzards Bay without incident, enjoying the scenery and calm water. By late afternoon, Angus had navigated our way to a small deserted island in Buzzards Bay and there we made camp for the night.

The next day was as bright and sunny as the one before and we congratulated ourselves on having such good weather. The day passed uneventfully, both of us enjoying the freedom of our thoughts as the little boat skimmed over the water. We continued on toward Providence, camping out again at the end of the day.

As we checked the course early on the morning of the fourth day, we realized we would be in Providence that night, on schedule. The Providence River empties into Narrangansett Bay almost 15 miles from Providence itself and most of the afternoon was spent leisurely cruising up the River. The sun was bright and strong once again. We took the opportunity to dry out wet clothing and relax from the morning's run when we had gotten wet in some tide rips going under the Mount Hope Bridge. Socks, shoes and shirts were now spread out on top of the gas cans in the bow.

We began to meet other boats coming down the river and exchanged friendly waves for curious looks. Most of the traffic consisted of luxury cabin cruisers and we thought our boat probably looked like a garbage scow.

"So who cares?" Angus said. "We've had more fun in the last four days than they'll have in a lifetime."

"You know it, Gus," I agreed.

The river became more and more narrow as we neared our destination. By late afternoon, we began to see large freighters tied up at the Providence piers. The ships looked huge from our vantage point and occasionally we noticed curious seamen looking over the rails from far up on the main decks.

It wasn't long before we realized we were going to have some problem finding a place to dock. All the landings were owned by someone and technically we would be trespassing if we were to pull in without permission. We found one with a few small cruisers and rowboats tied up and I decided to chance it.

"Let's pull in here and see what happens," I said.

I remember feeling a little queasy as the boat bumped against the wooden dock. I realized at once that that dull thump signaled the end of our trip.

"Well, old buddy, we made it." I said. "By Christ, we made it."

I reached forward toward Angus and we grasped each other's hand and held on firmly. We got out onto the dock and walked up a steep ramp to a little building at the end of a dirt path. There was a patio in back of the building with tables and chairs. We crossed the patio and went in through a low narrow doorway. Inside was a jukebox, more tables and chairs and a bar with a half-dozen elbow benders enjoying an end-of-the-day beer.

"All right if we leave our boat out there for a little while?" I asked the bartender.

"Guess so, if it ain't taking up too much space," he replied.

"It's only a rowboat," I said.

"Rowboat! Where you guys been? Look like you ain't seen land for weeks."

"We just came down from Boston," I said, trying to sound nonchalant. I wondered how we did look with four days of beards and no baths.

"Boston? Man, you pulling my leg?" he asked.

With that he went out to look for himself, followed by a few of his customers. He came back minutes later offering drinks on the house. We accepted the drinks and the accolades with equal pleasure.

Much later that night, Angus' father came down and loaded the boat, sailors and equipment into the truck. I was exhausted and tried to sleep. My thoughts went back over the last four days and all that had happened. I knew we had done something we would never forget, something grand, something important. We had planned it. We had pulled it off. And it had been a great success.

It would be ten years before I would be involved with boats again. My first boat was an old 28-foot Chris Craft with a single, six cylinder engine. She was 26 years old and so was I, and I always felt we at least had that in common. She was replaced two years later by a newer 28-footer that had twin six cylinders. Twin engines . . . that was arriving in boating, and I worked them to death learning how to maneuver with them to best advantage. Three years later, I replaced her with an almost new, 33-foot fiberglass boat with twin V-8 engines and a flying bridge.

They all kept me in the poorhouse but I only used them about 30 days out of the year and spent about 60 days a year working on them. And never a day went by without my asking myself, "Why?" I still don't have the answer, but I have a few ideas.

There are a lot of pithy sayings about men and their boats and one of the favorites, especially among the nonsympathetic wives and girl friends of boat owners, is: "You can tell a man's age by the price of his toys." But I submit that there is more to it than that. Certainly, there are some men of vast wealth who do own boats only as toys and often never so much as go aboard them and surely never take them to sea. However, I'm talking about the majority of small boat owners who buy second-hand boats and work their hearts and souls out on them and use them whenever they can.

Why do we spend our hard-earned money, put ourselves in hock and work our tails off owning and maintaining these boats which make us seasick, exasperated, exhausted, frightened and often alone, these machines which we love when they serve us well and loathe when they fail us?

There comes a time for many of us, I think, when we begin to realize how little control we have over our lives. We are killed in plane crashes or we survive an operation, we are promoted in our work or we are passed over, we are loved or we are forgotten. And day after day, we get up in the morning and go out to do the same thing we did the day before and come home at the same hour, watch the same news on television that we saw the night before and go to bed at the same hour. There is damn little in our lives and in our work that we can point to with pride and say, even if only to ourselves, "I did that, it's done well and I'm proud of it." Group think and group work is killing us as individuals.

And yet any half-baked, hundred-dollar-an-hour psychiatrist will tell you that personal pride and a sense of accomplishment and control over one's life are vital to us. We need these things like we need sex and food.

Now, take someone in this kind of morass and give him a boat. Let him examine every plank in the hull, every nut and bolt of it, every speck of paint, every wire, every pipe, every valve and let him go on to make every one of these things worthy of its existence. It is possible for an individual man to work on a boat and make it into a device which will function properly. He can then test and prove his ability by taking his boat before the elements and returning unscathed. You now have a man who has accomplished something, the total of which is noble and worthwhile and *he did it.* Boating may well be one of the last personal frontiers left to us: a chance to sign our name to something of our own, with pride.

I was astonished and flattered. The letter had come from St. Vincent, the next island south, and was signed by Ian Child, chairman of the Petit St. Vincent Race Committee. Would I, he had asked on the committee's behalf, consent to serve with *Visitor IV,* as committee boat for their annual Thanksgiving Race Week? For the hundredth time in the past month, I went down the jetty to Beverly's office to get her advice.

"Don't be too flattered, Bob," said Beverly with her usual frankness. "They need a big boat and can't afford to charter one and *Visitor* is the only big one around. They probably hope you'll be flattered enough to do it for expenses."

"Should I?" I asked.

"I think so. The trip will get you out of St. Lucia and into the rest of the islands. You'll meet some interesting people, see some of the real charter boats and you might even have a good time."

I went back to *Visitor* and dug out some charts. The trip would take me about 110 miles south via St. Vincent and

Palm Island to Petit St. Vincent, known to those in the area as PSV. The trip scared me. I had no deep water navigation experience, and, although the islands were so close I would almost never be out of sight of land, I had been around long enough to have heard horror tales of the seas in the channels between the islands. Also, there simply were no aids to navigation in the West Indies as we knew them. A light or bouy plotted on a chart might be there or it might not. Having a light depended mostly on whether or not the light keeper felt like turning it on that night.

And of course, I had little faith in *Visitor IV*. Some of the basics of restoring her to a safe and functional condition had been started but because there was no great hurry and because I was living aboard, I had placed emphasis on straightening up the inside living quarters. And a lot of time had been spent meeting hotel managers and staff to promote the boat for the coming season, as well as working with some friends back in Boston on a brochure and poster which I hoped to be able to distribute in the hotels.

Actually, I had always felt *Visitor*'s hull was sound, and her engines had been performing perfectly during the few times I had taken her out. But there were a lot of unanswered questions about her electrical and plumbing systems which bothered me. And frankly, I was a little ashamed of the way she looked. She still needed a fresh coat of paint and some varnish work outside and the inside varnish work was as black as the day I first saw it. Even the horrible indoor-outdoor carpeting was still in place. There had been no suitable new carpeting available in the shops in St. Lucia and I had been forced to order what I needed through a local merchant. While the colonial ties may have been broken with Britain, those of trade had not, and so my carpeting was coming sea freight from England. It took three months.

I had found someone to do upholstery work so my salon sofa had new foam rubber cushions and had been covered with a lovely new orange tweed. The wheelhouse bench seat had been covered in deep blue and I had new orange bedspreads. But oh, how I hated the sight of that institutional green, faded and stained indoor-outdoor carpeting.

My desire to get the old girl out on the water and see how she would do finally won out over my vanity and I wrote Ian accepting his kind offer with pleasure. He wrote back, almost at once, and gave me all kinds of friendly and helpful information on how to select the sailing time which would offer the smoothest channel crossing; where to anchor at St. Vincent, and better still, where not to; how to find him, and so on. I had the feeling I was going to like Ian Child and I was right.

There wasn't much time. I made a list of critical things to get done before leaving. It included changing the engine oil and the fuel and oil filters on both engines and the generator—a long, dirty, miserable job. I also tested the windlass by letting go the anchor at dockside and raising it up again. It worked just fine with the chain rattling out through the hawsepipe as though we were the QE2. Little did I realize how poor a test of chain windlass that was. I broke down all the battery connections and cleaned them with a wire brush and sandpaper and then washed the batteries down with baking soda and water. There were nine 100 amp hour batteries which some idiot had installed under the desk and the bunk in the main stateroom. Somehow, past owners of *Visitor* had survived sleeping over the fumes which all batteries generate, but I had future plans to relocate them in the engine room where they belonged.

Sailing day arrived too soon. I had been unable to get a balky fathometer to work well and the new charts I had ordered hadn't arrived. But we had a commitment, so sail we must. I told Ramshen, my crewman of less than a month, to spend the night on board because we would be getting an early start.

Ramshen was about 18 years old, an East Indian, the son of a shopkeeper in a nearby fishing village called Anse la Raye. He was a neat, happy, good-looking young man and, while he didn't do any work that he felt he could get away with avoiding, I would have been lost without him. I think he took a certain amount of pride in being the crewman on *Visitor IV*. She was the biggest yacht on the Island and I was to discover later

31

that working on her was considered a good job to have.

That afternoon, we moved *Visitor* to the fuel dock and, for the first time, I took on fuel. *Visitor* had two tanks of 150 gallons each and had a cross-connection pipe so that, for all practical purposes, she carried 300 gallons of diesel fuel. Her tanks were nearly dry and the fuel pump was a slow one, so I did what one should never do, even with diesel which is far less dangerous than gasoline. I put the fill nozzle in the tank fill pipe, turned it on and went off to do other things. Of course, I checked the pump meter occasionally, but it was a long way from 300 gallons.

"Mr. Bob! Mr. Bob! Mr. Bob!" Ramshen was moving down the fuel dock faster than I had ever seen him move and calling at the top of his lungs.

"De fuel she everywhere, everywhere!" he exclaimed.

I lunged for the pump and shut it off, astonished to see it reading 170 gallons. What a mess! Diesel fuel was running all over the deck, down the topsides, around the combing, into and all over the cockpit deck, down the cockpit hatch and into the bilge. It didn't seem possible. But it was, and the explanation on a neglected boat was simple enough. The crossover pipe was full of 30 years of gunk and would pass only a tiny bit of fuel at a time to the other 150 gallon tank. After the first tank had filled up, about 10 gallons had seeped through to the other tank and another 10 gallons had spread out all over the place.

It took two gallons of household detergent to clean up the mess, but we got it done, filled the other tank individually and got to bed in time for about four hours sleep. It was not an auspicious beginning.

I am not an astronomer and the phases of the moon have always seemed about as interesting to me as the time of day: you know it's there but you don't really know why. I was to learn on this trip that the moon affects the tide, the tide affects the size of the waves in the channels between the islands, and the size of the waves affects the flow of adrenaline in my veins, and that affects the amount of moisture in my mouth. And so I became interested in the phases of the moon.

Those more knowledgeable than I calculated for me that, owning to the particular phase of the moon on our departure date and taking into consideration a lot of other esoteric mumbo jumbo which I didn't understand, an 0600 (six o'clock in the morning) departure would insure a comparatively calm channel between St. Lucia and St.Vincent. I believed them and they were right.

By 0630, Ramshen, *Visitor IV* and I were sailing down the misty coast of St. Lucia. It was cold that early in the morning but the air was good enough to eat, the water calm, the engine exhaust purring quietly in back, the sky just beginning to lighten on the horizon. I had entrusted *Visitor* to the autopilot and Ramshen and I were sitting up front on the bow seat. We would spend several hours going down the coast before we would strike off on a course for St. Vincent. I spent the whole time on the bow and remember it as one of the best. There is really no finer time on a boat than the very early morning. The seas can be glassily calm sometimes and there is a quietness and peacefulness, a oneness with the water that goes away as the sun comes up. You have to be there to know it.

My thoughts drifted back 20 years to that first trip Angus Kennedy and I had made in his 11-foot boat with a 10-horse Johnson. Angus was dead now, killed in an automobile accident. How he would have loved to have seen *Visitor IV* and to have been aboard on this trip. The boat was a little different, but the spirit and emotions were the same as when he and I had set out that summer day so long ago.

I laid our course for St. Vincent from the Pitons and I noted the time as we turned onto it. Now we would find out what the channels were really like. I had been boating long enough to know that the other guy's description of wave height can often be compared to a fisherman's description of fish length. For the first hour or so it was really quite calm, but from then on the waves did begin to build and, after two hours, I cut the engines back so that we could ride more comfortably over two to three footers. Still nothing to worry about. It wasn't until we were within sight of the north end of St. Vincent that it really began to get rough. We wallowed around in five and six footers at 700 rpm, or about 6 knots, for several hours until we were able to make the lee of the Island. *Visitor* was an old boat and I had no intention of abusing her in rough seas.

I was tired from fighting the wheel and we were both hungry. The lee shore of St. Vincent was almost flat calm and it seemed a good idea to nip into Chateaubelair Bay and have a comfortable lunch before continuing down to the southern tip of St. Vincent and Kingstown Harbor, our destination. It was a mistake. We wasted too much time enjoying ourselves and even took time for a swim. It was 1630 when we were under way again and I figured we had about two hours to go. That would get us in just before dark, which was critical because I didn't know Kingstown Harbor and had been told not to rely on the navigational lights. As it was, it took three hours and, as we rounded up into the Harbor, the last rays of the sun slipped below the horizon.

I had a Harbor Chart which showed good range lights for entering. The only problem was they weren't lit. At least, I couldn't find them. The chart showed an anchorage in the northeast corner and I headed for that. I turned on the fathometer and waited for its ancient tubes to warm up. And waited. And waited. No. This was the time when it was needed and it wasn't going to work. I edged in close to the other anchored boats, picked a spot where I would have room enough to swing without hitting anyone else and stopped the boat. I went forward to my trusty windlass, freed the clutch and the brake, and let the anchor and chain drop. It ran out beautifully. I dashed back to the wheelhouse to put on a little sternway, as is proper in anchoring, and zipped forward again to tighten the brake and stop the chain. The chain was straight up and down and had stopped running out. And *Visitor* was still drifting backwards. Toward a half-dozen other anchored boats.

I knew what I had done. Without the fathometer, I had let the anchor go in very deep water and it wasn't holding. Zip back to the wheelhouse to check our sternway with the engines, zip up to the bow to start the electric winch to pick up the anchor and chain and then try again in another spot. The windlass would up a link of chain, gave an audible sigh, wound another link, gave a bright flash of light, a puff of smoke and died.

The next two hours were among the worst I was to spend on the Motor Yacht *Visitor IV*. In the first place, it began to rain. Hard. Visibility dropped to 200 feet. And it began to blow. Onshore. Hard. I dropped down into the crew's quarters and looked into the chain locker. All 250 feet of the stuff had run out. Back up on deck, I found I could not alone raise the chain by hand. Ramshen came to help and the two of us lifted about two feet of it and locked it into place on the teeth of the gypsy. By now we had drifted dangerously close to shore and the anchored boats, so I had to zip into the wheelhouse and jockey the boat out into the middle of the Harbor again. And so it went: foot by foot of wet slippery chain; pulling together, moving the boat again; pouring rain, driving wind; cold, exhausted.

Ramshen was getting weak. I could tell because, without his effort, I couldn't raise the chain at all. And there were times now when, although we were pulling together, it wouldn't move.

"Pull, goddamnit, pull," I shouted at him, and he tried again. And again he weakened and again I hollered at him. And again he tried. We had been at it for more than an hour, resting only long enough to relocate the drifting *Visitor IV*. We were soaked to the skin and our hands were raw and bleeding. I didn't see how we would ever get that chain aboard. I just couldn't pull again.

"Pull, goddamnit!"

Who had said it? I looked at Ramshen. Even in the darkness and rain, I could see the determination on his face. Christ! My damn crew was telling me to pull! God, how I pulled after that. And we did it. We got the anchor clear of the water. Nothing could ever have persuaded me to let it go again, so I nosed *Visitor* into the commercial dock where yachts were not really allowed and came alongside an old inter-island copra schooner. The skipper had evidently been watching the whole

35

show, for he beckoned us to tie alongside, an unheard-of courtesy between a hardworking schooner and a pleasure yacht.

I woke the next morning feeling as though I had been run over by a train. Everything I owned ached. I went to the customs office and cleared in, thanked the schoonermen, then brought *Visitor* out of Kingstown and around to the beautiful Young Island Anchorage where I was to meet Ian Child. Thanks to his good advice, and using the anchor line rather than chain, my second anchoring went rather well.

While waiting for Ian, I took the inspection plate off the electric motor of the windlass. The familiar burnt ozone smell told me the story. While it had been able to lift the ten or fifteen feet of chain I had let out while testing it back at Ganter's, 250 feet had been too much and the motor was burned to a crisp.

"Visitor IV! . . . Visitor IV! . . . Visitor IV!" I looked up to see some madman bearing down on me in a small boat, waving and calling at a great rate. After circling me twice, the boat came up to my boarding ladder and out of it sprang Ian Child. He turned out to be a man of boundless enthusiasm, dry wit, intelligence and grace. Looking back on the trip, meeting Ian Child was the highlight.

He talked incessantly about St. Vincent, the West Indies and the West Indian people. I learned a great deal from him which was helpful in the years to come. His house was situated in a veritable botanical garden of West Indian plants, trees, flowers, fruits and vegetables (West Indians call most vegetables "ground provision"), all carefully tended by his equally charming wife, Vivian. That night, I was treated to a West Indian dinner at their home which was superb. For dessert we had hot, stewed guavas spooned onto vanilla ice cream. I shall never forget it.

The Annual PSV Thanksgiving Race Week has three races: the first from St. Vincent to PSV; the second a more complicated course through the Grenadines, starting and finishing at PSV; and the third from PSV back to St. Vincent. Once the committee had started the first race at St. Vincent, they were to fly to Palm, the island nearest PSV that had an airstrip. I was to meet them there, and take them to PSV where we would establish the finish line. Timing was critical because, if the fastest entry were to reach the finish before we did, there wouldn't be a finish line.

I got an early start the next morning to make sure I would be on time to meet them. We headed south to little Bequia (pronounced Bek-qui), one of the true jewel islands of the area, and I was disappointed not to have time to stop. I did have several chances later, and its enchantment was never lost on me. Out in the channel between Bequia and Canouan, we came upon a school of playful porpoise and, again putting *Visitor* in the hands of her autopilot, I spent a fun-filled hour on the bow watching those incredible mammals jump and dive, criss-crossing in front of the bow at unbelievable speed. One jumped higher than the bow rail and actually grazed the rail as it fell back into the water.

We had made good time and, using Street's excellent *Yachting Guide to the Grenadines*, which laid out critical ranges for navigation, I took a shortcut through the Tobago Cays. To a novice, without Street's book, this complex of reefs and tiny, uninhabited islands would be a nightmare. There is not one man-made aid to navigation. For years, mariners have relied on natural ranges and Street has carefully documented the best of them. They are easily followed if you take your time and pay attention. Your reward is a trip through some of the most beautiful waters in the world.

It was a totally new experience for me and took some getting used to. In those waters, it wasn't unusual to see the bottom clearly in 20 or 30 feet of water. Where I had been boating, in Massachusetts Bay, if you see the bottom, it means only one thing: you're aground.

We dropped anchor in the little bay at Palm Island, well ahead of the plane and the committee. Ramshen and I had our first real chance to relax since leaving St. Lucia. It really seemed too soon when the little twin-engine chartered plane buzzed over us and touched down on Palm's grass landing strip, but when I looked at my watch, I realized they were behind schedule. By the time they and all their equipment had been ferried out to where we were anchored, time had become critical. We could actually see the sails of the lead boats on the horizon.

I fired up the engines and Ramshen started to take up the anchor line. Two or three of the committeemen went to help him. Something held them up and I left the wheelhouse to see what was the matter. Ian was there and was dumbfounded.

"Bloody thing just won't come up," he said.

Ramshen was over the side into the water in a moment and came back to the surface with the problem.

"De anchor she does be caught in de chain, Mr. Bob,"he said.

It didn't seem possible but we had managed to anchor near an old mooring block with a few feet of chain still attached. The chain had been picked up in the flukes of my Danforth anchor and was jammed tight against the stock, 35 feet down. I had learned long ago to keep diving gear on a boat and I am a qualified diver. There was nothing to do but get the gear out and go down and free the anchor.

The committee was in a state of panic by this time. I could hear a few muttered questions about the competency of the captain, but knew such comments could only come from those who had never operated a boat in their lives. Boating is the classic environment for Murphy's Law: If there is anything that can go wrong, it will. And all yachtsmen know it and have long since learned to roll with the punches.

In any case, it only took five minutes to free the damn thing. I went up to the wheelhouse still wearing my diving gear, hitched the old girl up hard and we were almost planing as we crossed the PSV channel on what fortunately had to be one of the calmest days. That little three-mile hop can be as nasty as they come. The finish line was set in time and the big puffers came across single file to receive their horn blast and stop the time clock.

Most of the entrants were area charter yachts and they raced for a needed change from the rigors of chartering. November was a quiet month and few, if any, risked losing business by taking time off. But there were some fine, locally owned yachts entered as well and they made an impressive assembly when they were all anchored at PSV.

I never really understood whether race weeks were for racing or for jump-up, but I do know the participants enjoyed both to the fullest. Jump-up was a broad term that covered all manner of jollification, including dancing, drinking, steel bands, drinking, singing, drinking, telling sea stories, drinking, protesting, drinking, fighting, drinking and having one hell of a good time. And getting drunk. It happened anytime between sundown and sunup and, at its very best included both, nonstop. PSV was a resort island that sponsored Race Week to help promote its name and business. Every evening during Race Week, they put on a grand feast for all comers, complete with a steel band, a bamboo flute band, contests and the like. It was jump-up at its best.

While no records were broken at jump-up that night on shore at PSV, no standards were lowered either. Being something of an amateur, I staggered my weary way back to *Visitor IV* at about two in the morning. As committee boat, I had been accorded the privilege of tying up overnight at the fuel dock. There were no other docks at PSV, so the race fleet was at anchor in the bay. I was asleep almost before my head hit the pillow.

It's a strange thing about boats. After being around them for a while, especially living aboard, if something goes wrong at night, you'll wake up. And I was suddenly awake. I stared at the overhead trying to figure out why. The wind had come up, I could hear it. But I was safely tied up and had no dragging anchor to worry about. *Visitor*'s starboard side was bumping against the dock but I knew the fenders . . . *Starboard side!* Christ, we were port side to and something was bumping my starboard side!

I was on deck in seconds wearing nothing but my undershorts. I couldn't believe what I saw. *Visitor* was surrounded by a forest of masts, hulls and rigging. The wind was blowing out of the west at a good 20 knots, not very strong, but enough to cause some ten or twelve sailboats that ranged in size from 20 to 42 feet to drag their anchors. And they had all, slowly but surely, piled up at the east end of the bay against the fuel dock, which was to say, against *Visitor IV*. Because they were dragging, everything had happened in slow motion and no real damage had been done. But what a mess. The first task was to wake the sodden owners who had slept through the whole thing and to get them out on deck. Bleary-eyed and with blossoming hangovers, we set to the task of untangling anchor lines, rigging, fenders, dinghies, nerves and tempers. Slowly, one boat at a time was freed enough for the owner to start the engine and power away from the mess. Within an hour, it was all sorted out and we were back catching the sleep we would need for tomorrow's race.

The wind had abated a bit by morning, but was still strong enough to promise an exciting race. I was anxious to put on a good show for the race committee after yesterday's fouled anchor and, as usual, they were late by the time I saw them coming down the fuel dock. Breakfast had been slow in coming and the hangovers slow in going.

I fired up *Visitor* and Ramshen did a better than usual job of taking in and stowing lines and fenders. I had a bit of a challenge on my hands because I wanted to back around the end of the fuel dock to put the bow into the wind. The race fleet was packed together in the anchorage and I was going to have to thread-the-needle to get through them. It was important to be lined up well with the wind before I got to them.

Therefore, I was doing some fancy twin-engine jockeying off the end of the fuel dock when the port engine stopped cold. There was something about the way it stopped that I didn't like so, with the wind ready to blow me back onto the dock, I hollered at Ramshen to get the anchor over. It turned out that I was in the soup again.

The day before, I had noticed that there was a smart 28-foot Striker sport fisherman tied stern to the end of the fuel dock. I had been told it belonged to the resort organization which owned PSV. What I had not noticed was that the Striker was not held off by her own anchor at the bow, as is customary in mooring stern to, but rather by a permanent mooring block and a piece of self-floating, one-inch plastic line. This was convenient because the boat came and went quite frequently from

40

her tie-up. Her crew simply picked up the floating line from the bow with a boat hook. Well, the Striker was off on some errand, and I had picked up the floating line with my port propeller.

Not only was I beginning to look like a complete fool, but worse, I was beginning to believe it myself. Ramshen, bless his heart, saved a small part of my shattered dignity by offering to go over the side with a diving mask and knife himself. Perhaps I looked the fool but at least I had a good crewman.

Bits and pieces of plastic line floated to the surface at the stern and the committee began to murmer. Fortunately, last night's excesses kept the noise level low. Five minutes later we were threading our way through the 50 or so anchored sailboats with what I thought was consummate skill. I hoped desperately that someone, at least one person, noticed.

The starting line was set up, the stopwatches wound and the starting flags readied. I watched the whole process with interest. Being a stinkpotter of many years standing, I had often wondered what sailing was all about and now I was getting a chance at least to watch. When the five minute flag went up, I climbed on top of the wheelhouse to get a better view and to get out of the way.

Visitor on anchor was, in effect, one end of the starting line; a flag on the near shore was the other end. The result was that when the final flag went up, a field of some forty sailing yachts zeroed in on my bow. Some of them were huge ocean racers more than 50 feet long. I had never seen such a frightening sight in 15 years of boating. My powerboat approach to sailboats is that they are basically out of control when under sail, and here they were bearing down on my poor *Visitor* like so many runaway locomotives.

The closer they got to me, the tighter they bunched and the tighter the knot in my stomach became. One beautiful blue ketch went right over my anchor line and the slack went out of it as the keel of the ketch caught and drew it tight. Later, when I took the anchor line in, I saw it had bottom paint on it. A different 42-footer was squeezed out of space in front of my bow by another boat and had to luff up into the wind to take

41

way off. He ended up alongside *Visitor*'s hull, dead in the water and a fender's width away. We could have tied him up and called it perfect docking. Somehow he caught the wind and got across the line, last.

The race was to take most of the day and so we hauled anchor and went back to the dock. All sorts of activities were planned for those who remained ashore, including sailfish races, greased pole contests, treasure hunts, beach jump-up and more.

I went up to the PSV resort office to apologize for cutting up the Striker's mooring line. They were good sports about it and had already replaced it, this time with a white float as well. It was in the resort office that I met Tom Vickery.

I knew of Tom because he was involved in the charter yacht radio network. Because charter yachts spend much of their time at sea, on anchor or at other locations where immediate communication is impossible, a radio net was set up some years ago wherein all yachts, charter agents and some other shore facilities tune a particular frequency, 2527 m Hz, during the day from 0800 to 1600. This is the only way, for example, that a charter agent can confirm a particular yacht's availability for a potential charter, as well as take care of the hundred and one other details that come up before, during and after the charter. Flight reservations for departing charterers, confirmation of bank deposits and other funds, emergency messages from home are just a few of the details handled by radio. Because the charter market for the West Indies covers the nearly 350 miles from Antigua to Grenada and radios, even the best of them, have not much more range than 75 to 100 miles, we all pitch in and help relay messages to distant locations.

Tom Vickery owned and operated the delightful Mermaid Tavern on the island of Carriacou but took pleasure in helping out with radio relay and used the call letters MTV for Mermaid Tavern Vickery. It should be pointed out that there was no Federal Communications Commission in the West Indies and we could do pretty much as we pleased. It was to the yachting community's credit that, in my experience, the marine frequencies were far less abused in our area than they were in the U.S.

In any case, I was delighted to meet Tom because I had heard him on the air many times and admired his professionalism in his use of his station. We talked about generalities and finally he asked me what I was doing in the area. I told him about *Visitor* and he asked me to show her to him. Actually, we could see her at the fuel dock from where we stood, so I pointed her out. Tom looked for a moment.

"For chrissake!" he exclaimed, and then went on more thoughtfully. "That looks . . . like . . . a yacht I used to know that was tied up in the '40s and '50s at the Cleveland Yacht Club . . . belonged to a guy named Roberts."

My mind began to dance. I couldn't believe what I was hearing. One of the little treasures I had found aboard *Visitor* in the liquor closet in the salon was a set of matched drinking glasses. They had the yacht's name on them and, above that, a pair of crossed flags. Even without having one before me, I could remember that one flag was a burgee with CYC on it and the other a swallowtail owner's flag with an R in the center. It seemed impossible. Nearly 2,500 miles away from where he had seen her and thirty years later, in the remotest part of the West Indies, a man with a photographic memory had recognized *Visitor* and had furnished that part of her history which no one there, not even Monty Robinson, had known . . . her original port and owner.

For Tom Vickery was right. When I got back to St. Lucia, I wrote to the Cleveland Yacht Club and got a nice letter back from the club secretary. Yes, *Visitor* had been there for nearly twenty years and was remembered still by many present club members. In fact, her owner, Warren K. Roberts had been an officer in the club several times and the letter included his last known address in Florida. I wrote to Mr. Roberts at that address but never received a reply. I could only asume he was no longer living. I was disappointed because I would have liked to have found out *Visitor*'s route from the Great Lakes to the Caribbean.

Visitor had had only four other owners: one who had

43

brought her to St. Thomas and chartered her there; another who had taken her farther south to Barbados where Monty Robinson had purchased her and brought her to St. Lucia; and, of course, myself. The old girl had come a long way.

The finish of a sailboat race is a bit anticlimactic unless you are one of the racers or otherwise more involved than I was. They cross the finish line one at a time, often with long periods in between. It is the duty of the Committee to wait for the very last boat, for all must be timed. There can be some excitement when the occasional protest flag is unfurled, but our committee members were all pros and did their job well. There were no justified protests, so the times were announced and the winners went off to celebrate.

I have never felt particularly at home among sailors, and I'm sure they have never felt very comfortable among power boaters. The day's pros and cons, the battles won and lost could not keep my attention that evening. I went back to *Visitor* with the thought of eating dinner aboard. As I stepped down into the galley, it smelled as though dinner were waiting. Ramshen was in front of the stove tending a boiling pot. It smelled superb. "Whatcha cooking?" I asked. "Does be fish and brof and green fig, Mr. Bob." He offered me some and we had a fine dinner of boiled dolphin, onion, Ramshen's selection of spices and "green fig", which was green banana. I remembered, as we ate and talked, Monty Robinson's admonition: "Never take one's meals with them." I wouldn't have missed dinner with Ramshen that evening for anything.

Later that night, a fine old boat went to her grave. I was awakened by a commotion on the dock, got dressed and went out to investigate. It seemed that an old 98-foot Baltic Ketch, which I had seen in St. Lucia several weeks before, had been coming down with the charterers to see Race Week. Her skipper had made two classic mistakes in these waters: he had chosen to sail down the windward side of Canouan Island and he had done so at night. Because the wind sets a sailing craft to its lee side, a boat sailing down a windward coast runs the risk of being set in toward shore. Of course, during the day, the skipper can tack away from the shore if he gets too close. Still, it's a risky business in a Baltic Ketch, not the most agile of craft, and pure foolishness to try it at night.

She was carrying nine passengers and a crew of three. The wind was strong and the swell worse. Most of her passengers were seasick, wet and miserable. The skipper made his final mistake when he changed course in an attempt to make the boat ride better and his passengers a little more comfortable. He turned west when he estimated that he was past the southern tip of Canouan, expecting to put the seas on his stern. Twenty minutes later, a particularly big swell picked up the boat and set it down with a stomach-wrenching crash on the well-charted reef which runs along the entire southern shore of Canouan.

The first crash broke the rudder. The second swell dropped the poor thing on its keel and broke her back. From there on, impaled on the reef, she was pounded by each succeeding swell. The sad loss of a fine old boat could have also been the tragic loss of 12 lives had it not been for the radio on board and the courage of a lone charter yacht skipper. The boat's distress call was picked up by incredible luck. PSV just happened to have its radio on and manned at that late hour because some radio traffic was expected. Normally, everyone goes off the air at 1600.

The alarm went out at once and the Trinidad Coast Guard patrol boat, which was at PSV for Race Week, was under way in minutes. I knew that at night, without a working fathometer, without radar and experience in those waters, for me to get under way would probably only mean that two boats would be in trouble. I went up to my wheelhouse and turned on the radio. The ketch was coming in loud and clear and the skipper was on the air. He sounded surprisingly calm. The water was waist-deep in the salon, he told us; she was heeled over about 20 degrees and a mast had snapped. Everyone was on deck but it was awash with waves as the swell broke over her. It sounded like absolute hell and I guess it was.

The Trinidad Coast Guard was on the scene in about 20 minutes. They got in as close as they dared and launched their Boston Whaler. Obviously, the only thing to be done was to rescue the survivors. There were painful periods of silence on the radio but we could follow most of what was happening. The whaler got in close and promptly hit some coral with its prop, shearing the pin and putting the boat adrift. They evidently didn't have any spare shear pins aboard.

By now, a cruising trimaran, the most unlikely of rescue vessels, arrived on the scene with one of the coolest-headed skippers in the Caribbean in command. He anchored up wind and, with his comparatively shallow draft, fairly close to the stricken ketch. He then secured a long piece of nylon line to his Zodiac, a superbly constructed rubber life raft which makes a popular dinghy in the West Indies because of its light weight and portability. This he launched and allowed to drift with the wind and waves down on the ketch. In spite of the six to eight foot swells, three survivors were able to jump into the Zodiac. The skipper of the tri then simply pulled them to his boat. In this way, with several trips, all were rescued. They were later transferred to the Coast Guard cutter and brought back to PSV.

Incredibly, no one had been injured. But a lovely old boat had been lost due to carelessness and stupidity, and that kind of loss is tragic. When a boat goes down because of age, or in a storm, or in spite of the courageous and competent efforts of her captain and crew, it doesn't seem quite so bad. However, with this kind of loss, no one wants to talk about it. There were no late night retellings of the tale that night. We simply got the survivors tucked into spare beds and the rest of us quietly went to bed ourselves.

The next day, we started the race back to St. Vincent without incident—no fouled anchors or propellers, no close calls at the start. We took the committee back to Palm Island to catch the waiting plane for the trip to St. Vincent, where they would establish the finish line.

From there, we headed back ourselves, having the fun of catching up with the racing fleet, boat by boat, and cheering each on as we went by. As we passed Canouan, we could see the masts of the Baltic Ketch showing above the water in the distance. They were tilted at about 40 degrees and looked very forlorn. I learned later that by the next day they were gone from sight.

We were well-anchored at Young Island, St. Vincent, by the time the first boat crossed the finish line. It had been an exhausting week. While anyone who had had some experience with all that had gone on during the past five days would have taken it all in his stride, it had been a lot for me. Only three months ago, I had been sitting behind a desk doing nothing and my boating experience had been limited to Massachusetts Bay with my little 32-footer. I decided to take the rest of the day off. I told Ramshen to do the same and, after he had cleaned up and changed his clothes, I took him ashore to St. Vincent in the dinghy.

I had heard a lot about the beauty of Young Island which lay the other side of the anchorage and thought it would be a good place to get some peace and quiet. How right I was. I tied my little dinghy to their dock and went ashore. Young Island was very small, only 20 acres, and consists, like PSV, entirely of a resort hotel. The buildings were nestled in lush, dense tropical foliage and there were delightful flagstone paths leading everywhere. Walking about, you had to duck your head to avoid a blossom covered frangipani branch or brush aside bougainvillaea heavy with burgundy flowers. The beach was as magnificent as the foliage but in its own way: long, white and flawless, broken only by occasional palm trees. Two of these were close together and a wide rope hammock had been strung between them. The temptation was too much. I climbed in, stretched out and gave it enough of a nudge to start it swaying. I looked out at the anchorage and saw my *Visitor* sitting proudly on the deep blue water, tugging slightly at her anchor line in the bit of current that was running. The sky was a superb blue with just a snow-white cloud or two to make it interesting. I turned to look the other way and saw a tall, distinguished-looking black man standing next to me. He wore an immaculate white shirt, deep red cummerbund and black pants. He was carrying a tray and a white towel.

"Can I get you something, sir?" he asked.

I thought a drink would make this perfect place into paradise.

"Yes," I said "And would you choose something for me? I don't care what it is as long as it's good, tall and cold."

"I know what you want," he said with a smile and started back toward the hotel's beach bar.

He was back in minutes with just what I had asked for except that it was the most magnificent drink anyone could imagine. I stayed in that hammock and that fine gentleman brought me four more coconut cows, as they were called, during the rest of the afternoon, without being asked. Never have I had more pleasure in giving a ten dollar tip. And never have I enjoyed an afternoon so much. That all too brief time will be a part of me for the rest of my life. I was still in the hammock when the sun set.

Ramshen showed up the next morning, looking a little sheepish, and I suspected his time ashore had not been all quietness and relaxation, as mine has been. It was time to head for the barn and, as I fired up *Visitor*'s engines, Ramshen went to work on the anchor line. We were under way by ten o'clock. I felt we were all right because I knew St. Lucia's coast and Castries Harbor by now, and, if we were delayed past darkness, there would be no problems such as we had had in Kingstown.

As we neared the north end of St. Vincent, it occurred to me that I had not thought to consult anyone about the best time to be crossing the channel. Well, too bad. We were on our way and we would just have to see what happened. I had a little more faith in *Visitor* by now, to say nothing of myself, and I certainly wasn't going to turn back to check on the phases of the moon. Ten minutes later, we were in it.

The waves came from every direction. They were eight to ten feet and we were to ride over some which were far higher than that. Engines idling at 500 rpm, we spent an exhausting five hours simply picking out the next big one, heading right into it, up and over and down into the trough long enough to pick up the course for a minute or two, and then there would be another that had to be met head-on or we'd be rolled over. The

48

seas were so confused that it wasn't always possible to pick the right wave and I saw my inclinometer stop between 35 and 40 degrees more times than I would expect anyone to believe.

Five or six times the salt water cooling pump on the port engine lost its prime. Then, the exhaust would sound as if an airplane were overhead and the fresh water cooling temperature gauge would start to climb. But, somehow, it would pick up again in a minute or two. The thought of having to shut down an engine in those seas was frightening but fortunately, it never came to that.

After five hours, the famous Pitons of St. Lucia came into view and the water calmed considerably. When we were well in the lee of St. Lucia, I turned the wheel over to Ramshen, who by now had become a fairly good helmsman, and I went below to look around and put things back in order. There was too much water in the bilges and I put the pump on the line. There were three separate bilges on *Visitor* with a valve manifold which could put the pump on any of the three. I lined up the engine room first and switched the pump on. Even with the roar of the engines, I could hear the high-pitched whine of a dry pump impeller. I shifted to the stern bilge, but she pumped for about a minute and went dry again. A little panicky, I shifted to the forward bilge with the same results. A check with a flashlight told me all three bilges were full of water and overflowing the stopwater floor timbers which separated them.

Of course, I didn't know how fast we were taking on water, but it didn't seem to be out of control. It was not rising noticeably, but there was a lot of it just the same and the pump was not pumping. We were an hour out of Castries and I could see nothing to do but keep going.

By the time we finally tied up at our dock at Ganter's, the water was up another inch which wasn't much in a 57-foot hull. But we were leaking and needed a pump.

I was able to borrow one from the marina and pumped her dry. The leak was easy to find then. All the kicking around in the St. Vincent channel had loosened a hull plank at the stern

49

and there was a neat little stream coming in. I felt we would be still afloat by the next morning, so I sent Ramshen home and went to bed myself, exhausted again but pleased that the trip had gone as well as it had.

After all, the anchoring problems were partly bad luck, inexperience and old equipment. Winding up the mooring line wasn't too bright, but it happens to the best of us once in a while. I had taken a 57-foot boat to sea, navigated her some 250 miles, at times through some of the trickiest reefs in the area, been a reasonably good committee boat, met my commitments, fought the worst seas by far that I had ever seen and gotten back safe and sound. Actually, I felt pretty damn good.

The tourist season was only a few months away, but there was enough work to be done on *Visitor* to keep a shipyard busy for a year. Or at least it seemed that way. The first job was that damnable bilge pump and by ten o'clock the morning after our return, I had taken it apart, found nothing wrong and put it back together. It still didn't work. That was when Peter McDoom had arrived. Peter, it turned out, was captain of a 60-foot motor launch belonging to the large resort hotel at the southern end of St. Lucia and he knew his boats and his mechanics.

He disconnected the pump suction pipe and replaced it with a length of hose which was lying loose in the engine room. The free end he stuck in the bilge water which, during the night, had reached an alarming height again. He turned the pump on and, of course, it began to suck water as though there were no tomorrow.

"Very simple, old man," he said as he came out of the hatchway. "Check two things. One, I'll bet the bilge strainers on the end of all three suction pipes have eroded away and,

51

two, those pipes are packed solid with all the crap loosened from the bottom of the bilges by the boat washing around in rough seas.''

What can I say? He was right on both counts. As I traced out the lines to find the strainers, I was appalled at the junk that lay in the bottom of the bilges. In places it was six inches deep. The bilges hadn't been cleaned in 20 years. The forward suction had no strainer on it at all. The other two were just as Peter had suspected: the mesh screens were gone and only the frames remained.

I took the two frames to the marina repair shop and asked them if they could fabricate a third one from scrap brass plumbing and braze on new screens. They could.

Ramshen and I spent the rest of the day head down and tail up in the engine room while I disassembled and cleaned out piping and he, with a kitchen serving spoon and a bucket, cleaned bilges. It is the gospel truth that he filled a ten quart bucket three times with oily bits of trash, rusted hose clamps, tools, engine parts, nuts, bolts, screws, gaskets and who knows what else. By day's end, we had a clean bilge and a working pump system.

I think in any situation, it takes time before a newcomer is accepted. Many people saw Ramshen and me working that day, covered from stem to stern with oil, dirt and grease as we carried our buckets of bilge slop to the trash area. I'm sure they began to think then that we were going to do what was needed to make *Visitor* a yacht to be proud of, no matter what it might take to do it. Our acceptance around Ganter's seemed to grow by leaps and bounds after that day.

Ross Donovan appeared out of nowhere the next morning as I was having breakfast. I had seen Ross around before but had been too busy to talk. One of Ross' sterling qualities, I was to learn, was that he rarely said anything unless there was something to say. Ross' uniform of the day consisted of a pair of orange swim trunks and flip-flops, those rubber sandals named after the noise they make when worn. I never saw Ross wear anything else during the day except when he occasionally took Beverly to lunch in town.

He was a good-looking man of average size and build with a bit too much gut. You couldn't help but like him because he never had a bad word for or about anyone. I never once saw him angry and he always had time to come and help with anything that needed doing.

No one, not even Beverly, who knew him best, really knew the story on Ross. He was a Canadian and lived alone aboard the unused boat which belonged to Gracie's silent partner. There seemed to be a kind of understanding that Ross was to keep an eye on it in return for having a place to live. Rumor had it that he was married and had children, but no one really knew and Ross never said anything about his personal life to anyone. Ross was just there and Ganter's wouldn't have been Ganter's, if he weren't. Ross' smiling face appeared at one of the salon windows as he rested his arms on the life rail.

"Morning," he said.

"Morning, yourself," I replied and offered him a cup of coffee. Ross, it turned out, had heard about my leak and wanted to know what I was going to do about it. I said that I really didn't know. I had heard of packing sawdust around the area from outside the hull, in the water, but that didn't sound like something for the long haul. Ross agreed and showed me what he had brought with him: a two part epoxy filler that could be applied under water, to wet surfaces. It had been around a long time, but I had never heard of it. Even when I saw it, I found it hard to believe that such a substance would work. But it did and it stopped my leak, absolutely bone-dry, with the help of four new screws to refasten the plank at the transom. Once again my scuba diving skills came in handy. I even packed some into the screw holes to cover the screws and protect the bare wood from woodworms.

That was the first of hundreds of times when Ross' ingenuity and know-where-to-find-it would save my neck in the months and years to come. That epoxy filler couldn't be had for love or money anywhere in the West Indies, but Ross had some when it was needed.

53

I knew that painting *Visitor* was going to be an enormous job and one that I didn't want to tackle. For one thing, my talents could be better used repairing, rebuilding and promoting the boat. Beverly had suggested that I should talk to George. George was a St. Lucian and a gentlemen and a fisherman and an honest-to-goodness yacht painter, in that order. He was, I guessed, in his fifties, Beverly said sixties, but as tall, lean and muscular as an Olympic athlete. George had worked hard all his life and was proud of every day of it. He had his own house and his own fishing canoe and Johnson outboard motor.

George had an indefinable way of being polite without sounding like an Uncle Tom although some of his companions accused him of just that. He could be respectful and at the same time tell you that you were going about it the wrong way. And somehow, mostly by hanging around Ganter's when the fishing was poor, he had learned how to slide a piece of sandpaper and lay a paintbrush. But George's unique claim to fame among his fellow St. Lucians was that if he said he would do some particular thing at some particular time, he did just that. And in this way, he had his competition beat cold. The favorite St. Lucian expression in response to being asked when something could be done was "just now", which meant anything from in five minutes to five years time. George said that he could sand, undercoat and finish coat *Visitor* from the water line to the top of her signal mast and that he could do it in one month, "God willing, Mr. Bob." And that was exactly what he did.

Two and a half years later when I wanted to spruce up *Visitor* to sell her, I again called on George and said simply that I wanted her painted again. I went away from St. Lucia for three weeks on other business. When I got back, the job was done.

I got in George's way from time to time while he worked on the painting. Someone had rigged up the damnedest arrangement on *Visitor*'s cabin top that involved wooden frames which boxed in the top surfaces so that they would catch rain water. The salon top, wheelhouse top and the midships deck area also had these crazy cisterns and they were all interconnected by a variety of multicolored lengths of garden hose which were finally joined at a point where the fresh water tank fill pipe was located.

I never speculated on the mentality of the individual who installed this mess. I was too busy ripping it out fast enough to keep ahead of George's sandpaper and brush.

I also removed from the otherwise useless midships deck area, two huge, unused storage lockers which took up the whole space. These had been installed with yacht-building craftsmanship and were of solid mahogany. Their removal was no small task. But when they were gone, and some deck stanchions which Ross had found somewhere were installed with safety lines, I had a whole new area for passengers. I ordered some deck chairs for the area and it was to become a favorite for sun bathers. George refinished the deck surface with white nonskid paint.

It was on this deck that the signal mast was stepped. That was all right. What was incredible was that, lashed to the mast near its base, were the yacht's two propane gas tanks, out in the open, knocking against the mast, unsightly and exposed to the elements. I again wondered what made people do the things they did with boats.

A young man living on a cruising sailboat at anchor in the harbor had been looking for work as a shipwright. I put him to work fashioning a proper and well-ventilated cabinet in a corner of my new sun deck, up against the wheelhouse. It would accommodate two propane tanks, protected, secure and out of sight. He used the wood from the large storage lockers which I had removed, and even put a small molding around the top surface, making it an excellent place from which to serve drinks and food to those on the sun deck. We got it finished just in time for George to apply two coats of primer.

Visitor's electrical system continued to make me nervous and so while George and Ramshen worked on the painting, I began to check out wires. St. Lucia's shore power was 220-

volt, single-phase AC, 50-cycle, which presented all sorts of problems for a boat designed and equipped for 110-volt, 60-cycle power. The refrigeration and air conditioning had had to have special transformers to compensate for the AC 50/60 cycle difference and these had been installed with the equipment. But the 220 volts had to be reduced to 110 and, being single-phase, the only method was to use a set of three large, expensive reduction transformers. These Monty Robinson had purchased some time ago and had installed under the eaves of the marina building. He had hooked them up to an already overloaded circuit of the marina's power panel, on the supply side of a 10-amp circuit breaker. The transformers had a combined capacity of 30 amps. From the transformers, he ran some 100 feet of extension cord to the boat. This terminated at an unprotected male connection.

When *Visitor* returned to the dock, it had been Monty's way to pick up this live connection and carry it on board and up onto the bow. He then got on his knees, leaned over the deck and chucked the connection through an open porthole in the crew's shower. "You have to be a little careful doing this," Robinson had advised me with great seriousness. He would then go inside to the crew's quarters shower and push the connector into a female receptacle mounted on the bulkhead which also carried the shower head. The two devices were about a foot apart. The cable from the female receptacle ran down the bulkhead, in between the shower stall base and the bulkhead, and finally, into the space below the floorboards. It then continued aft, alternately lying in the bilge water and rising up over floor timbers, until it reached the 110-volt power distribution panel.

To those of you with some knowledge of electrical apparatus and its care and feeding, I swear to you that the foregoing is the gospel truth.

I had seen all this when I had first come to St. Lucia to buy *Visitor*, and so, on my return, I had with me a complete set of Hubbel marine cable and connectors. It didn't take long to find a free 30-amp circuit breaker on the marina's panel and wire in my new 30-amp shore power cable. This I ran down the dock in a protected channel, then attached a new Hubbell connector. Its recessed counterpart I installed outside in *Visitor*'s hull, out of the way of spray and weather, and ran 30-amp cable from that receptacle into the engine room. There, I mounted on the aft bulkhead, near the air intake for cooling, the three reduction transformers which in turn were wired to the 110-volt distribution panel.

Visitor was not only reasonably safe, now, she also had her transformers with her when she went to other islands with 220-volt shore power.

My next project was to replace that god-awful propane hot water heater with the neat little electric job that I had had shipped to St. Lucia with some of my personal effects. The old unit came out easily enough, but I wanted to conceal the new one under the galley counter to save space and that became a three-day project. When everything was buttoned up and finished, I never saw that heater again and it served me without fail for three years.

One of the things I was having trouble teaching Ramshen was proper line tying and handling. *Visitor*'s dock was easy to approach and with her twin engines, she was a joy to maneuver. But I still wanted her tied up smartly and properly when we came in. So, when a character named Cracker came sauntering down the dock, I listened to what he had to say.

"Hey cap, what I mean to say, you need any splicin' done, any little bit o' canvas you need sew because I be a sailmaker and dat does be me trade and I doin' it plenty years now all de way from Barbados to Trinidad. Cracker me name, cap. Now you see dat piece o line dere? You fixing to throw it away? Let me show you just so. Twist de line so and you see de heart. De heart be good. Look there. That a good line. Plenty of use in that line. I know because I a sailmaker and dat does be me trade. I ain't like these limers you see here, man, I does a day's work and I gets me a day's pay. I buy me a little fish, some fig . . ."

Cracker loved to talk. He drove everyone else crazy but I loved to listen to him. He rarely had anything to say, but his words rang with bits of St. Lucian patois, Barbadian, Trinidadian and other West Indian accents. While others thought him a nuisance, I knew he had a good heart. He just liked to talk too much.

He could splice and I could not, at least not as well as he, and so between the two of us, we worked up a set of permanent mooring lines for *Visitor*. There was no tide to speak of at Ganter's, so each line could be made a fixed length with a spliced loop at the boat end and the dockside end permanently spliced to its dock cleat. Thus, all Ramshen had to learn was the right sequence of lines and how to drop the loops on the right cleats on *Visitor*. This he did, and many charterers in the months to come were to comment on how well Ramshen and I handled the old girl. And it always made me feel good when they did.

Fifteen years of boating has given me a healthy disrespect for many of the companies which manufacture equipment for the marine industry. I won't dwell on that. My shattered faith was, however, to be shored up slightly by the Ideal Windlass Company. Right after we had gotten back from Race Week, I had taken their name and address from the nameplate of my burned-up windlass and had written to ask if they could supply me with a new set of field coils for my unit. Bear in mind that this antiquated thing had been installed on *Visitor* more than 30 years ago. I didn't really expect a reply but, if I did get one, I felt sure it would be full of "We are terribly sorry to advise, etc."

A week had gone by when I received a package in the mail. From Ideal Windlass. With a new set of field coils. The right ones. And an invoice for $7.58. I couldn't believe it. Not only had they received my letter, forwarded through two address changes the company had had in the intervening years, but they had had the part, the right part, at a reasonable price, and had shipped it, air mail, well packaged, at once and on credit rather than asking for prepayment. Well, there was hope.

With my windlass back in order, I wanted to give some attention to the anchor chain. I had Ramshen pull out all 250 feet and found it badly rusted and without fathom markings. Even though I had known there was a lot of chain because I had lifted every damn link aboard that one wild night, I was still surprised to see *Visitor*'s water line come four inches out of the water at the bow when the chain had been stretched out on the dock.

Ross sauntered by and looked at the rusty mess.

"How you going to clean that?" he asked. I had been thinking about gallons of rust remover and a gross of wire brushes.

"Tell you how it's done," said Ross. "Borrow Beverly's car, hook the chain to the bumper and tow it about a mile down the road and back. It'll look like new."

Can't stand people like that. Just too damn smart. It worked like a charm and, by that afternoon, I had fathom marks painted on it. After letting the paint dry overnight, Ramshen and I pulled it back aboard with the windlass, wiping it lightly with an oily rag as it went. Progress.

Twice a day, I had *Visitor* all to myself; in the early morning, when I quite often had a lingering cup of coffee sitting out back in the cockpit, and in the evening, when I would drink Mt. Gay Rum and listen to my classical music on the new high fi system that I had installed. During the day, *Visitor* was a madhouse of activity. I remember that, at one point, there was a gal working on the upholstering; George was painting; Cracker was repairing a side curtain for the cockpit; another fellow was taking measurements for some new bow cushions; Fredrick, the owner of the engine repair shop, was checking out the injectors on the generator; and an old character called Yankee was lettering the transom; Ramshen was sanding varnish; and I was talking to the social director of one of the hotels about rates for groups.

It wasn't always like that, of course, but I did learn to cherish my moments alone. On one such morning, I was sitting out in back with my coffee when the strangest sight came into Vigie Creek from the Harbor. It was a 68-foot trawler yacht being towed by a 15-foot Boston Whaler with a 40-horsepower outboard. I wouldn't have thought it could have been done if I hadn't seen it myself. He was headed straight for the fuel dock. As he got closer, I recognized the boat as one I had seen a few days before in Marigot Bay, about seven miles down the coast from Castries.

He kept on coming for the fuel dock and I thought, "Christ, he's going to tow it right alongside!" There was clearly no one else aboard the trawler, so I dropped my coffee and ran for the dock. He seemed to have her lined up about right and was just passing the end of the fuel dock with the whaler when I got there. He had about 20 feet of towline and that huge, heavy trawler was moving at two or three knots. Too fast, even if it did clear the end and glide down the side of the dock as the fellow in the whaler obviously wanted it to do.

But it didn't clear. A little gust of wind began to blow just enough to give the trawler about six feet of leeway to starboard and she landed stem on to the end of the dock with a resounding crash. Well, two knots isn't all that fast and she was one of those rugged west coast boats. Her stem and metal cap had good dents in them and there was about a three-inch deep vee-shaped notch in a dock timber. The chap in the whaler turned out to be the trawler's skipper and the two of us got her tied up without too much trouble.

Later on, I asked him what had happened. Evidently, he had woken up early that morning and, rather than putting his feet on the shag carpeting of the crew's quarters floor, had put them into two feet of Marigot Bay water. He had anchored very close to shore with a bow anchor out and a stern line to a coconut tree, as is common in these parts. A seacock had failed in the night and the yacht had slowly settled to the bottom. It was his good luck that he had had her in shallow water. But starter motors, generators, alternators, transformers, air conditioning, refrigeration and who knows what else were soaked with salt water. Fortunately, her builder had known how to install batteries properly so that they were higher than the water in the engine room as was a main bilge pump. The skipper had been able to pump her out and make a temporary repair to the seacock. The only way to get her to Ganter's for the major repairs had seemed to be to tow her. I didn't bother to point out that a decent power yacht like mine could have done the tow job much more safely.

It later served as an impressive example of what apparently unlimited money can do. The skipper flew out that day for the west coast of the United States and was back in a week with all the replacement parts he needed. He brought them back excess baggage, first class, and spent several hundred dollars to breeze them through customs. He could have ordered everything by phone in Miami, but his girl friend lived in San Francisco and he hadn't seen her in a long time. His owner paid for the works.

Us poor folks at Ganter's received two gifts as a result of the accident. One was that we all ate the finest tenderloin steak for weeks, until it came out of our ears. With the refrigeration gone, the trawler owner's tremendous frozen steak supply was doomed and the Ganter's gang were the beneficiaries. Secondly, because other people's lessons are the least expensive, I went to work installing a bilge alarm on *Visitor IV*.

One of the little plusses I hadn't known about when I had bought *Visitor* was "the locker", although I had known it was there: an 11 by 12 foot room, one of many available to yacht owners at Ganter's for a handsome monthly rental. Monty Robinson had rented it for years and when I had seen it, it had been filled with the most incredible collection of junk imaginable. Debris was piled high in every corner, on shelves on one wall, and on a work bench on another. I had kept it because I had known I would need the work space. What I had not known about was the treasure-trove of spare parts, equipment, supplies and hardware hidden in amongst all the junk.

I had heard for months about Monty Robinson's former role in entertaining the officers of visiting warships. It seemed that good old Monty would, usually uninvited, go aboard any British or Canadian warship calling in St. Lucia, and offer to take the officers out for a day cruise, free rum punch, the lot, at no charge. Just good old Monty doing his bit for "our chaps".

He'd show them the time of their lives, all the while alert to

61

which one was the Supply Officer, which the Chief Engineer, and so on. At the end of the day, the customary pleasantries would run: " I say, old boy, a lovely day you've given us . . . can't tell you how much we appreciated it." Well, of course, they could do just that and Monty would be Johnny-on-the-spot. To the Chief Engineer he might say, "Well, old man, you know my port starter motor has been a bit off lately, you don't suppose one of your chaps . . ." To the Supply Officer he might say, "Well, you know, one can't imagine how difficult it is to get ¾-inch nylon line here in the colonies . . ."

I found out later from Ross that Monty had sold off most of the really valuable things he had had in the locker after I had bought *Visitor*, but before I had moved to St. Lucia. There was still an invaluable supply of small things left and, one weekend, I went through the lot of it and sorted out and threw out. And so, I knew I had a brand new bilge alarm on hand, courtesy, no doubt, of Her Majesty's Navy and intended for use in one of the ship's tenders. It went into *Visitor* the very afternoon of that day when the stricken trawler was towed into the fuel dock. Fortunately, I never heard it ring, but I was always glad to know it was there.

There was another story about Monty's reputation as benefactor to Her Majesty's Navy that always gave me a laugh. I had been in St. Lucia about four months when I received a call from no less than the office of the British Government Representative: Would I come and meet the Assistant B.G.R.? Well, I felt a bit slighted that I had been requested to meet with only the Assistant, but allowed as how I would be delighted.

I arrived promptly for my ten o'clock appointment and was shown into his office. The Assistant B.G.R. sat behind a rather tatty old desk surrounded by walls the color of the in-door-outdoor carpeting on *Visitor IV*. He was all smiles and handshakes and pleasantries. The conversation dragged on about nothing until he made his first mistake.

"I want you to know how delighted I am," he bubbled, "to hear that you are continuing the fine traditions with *Visitor IV* that Monty Robinson had established."

"I had rather hoped that that was one thing that I could avoid doing," I replied. Years of government service had trained him not to listen to what people replied and he went on without missing a beat.

"Perhaps you knew, Mr. Woodbury, about Monty's kindness and generosity in the past concerning our warships when they called at St. Lucia."

I said that I was aware of his freeloading, but again I was not heard. He went on to say that a British corvette was due in St. Lucia next week.

"The British Government Representative has asked me," he said as though he were speaking for the Queen herself, "to ask if you would like to take a group of officers out for a day on *Visitor IV.*" That was his second mistake.

I had spent five years in the American Navy as an enlisted man and remembered well the official wining and dining that was extended to officers when we came into a foreign port. The streets, bars and B-girls were left to the enlisted men. I told him that under no circumstances would I entertain the officers on *Visitor*.

"I'll tell you what I will do,"I said. "I'll round up a half a dozen wives and girl friends from the gang at Ganter's and your office can supply us with five cases of beer and I'll take as many as 25 (that was all *Visitor* could carry with the girls) enlisted men from that corvette, take them down to Marigot Bay, turn the high fi up full blast, put the swimming ladder over and stay there until the beer's gone. How about that?"

I never heard another word from the office of the British Government Representative.

George was finishing up the painting, and *Visitor* hardly looked like the same boat. I asked him to paint a deep blue, eight-inch wide stripe down both sides of *Visitor*, following the line of her sheer. He used the same color on the windlass, anchor chocks, and porthole rims. Later, when we hauled her to do the bottom, we used it for the boot top.

I had been asking around about someone who could letter the transom and, one day, an old fellow showed up at the end

63

of my dock. He said he had come to letter the transom. I was pretty skeptical. He looked scruffy, even dirty, and his clothes were worn almost to rags. He spoke without any trace of a West Indian accent. While I was curious about him, I wasn't going to let him near the transom unless I was sure he knew what he was doing. Lettering is an art.

"Listen Yankee," I said. I never did find out where he got that unlikely name. "Do you really know how to letter?"

"That's not the question," he replied. "The question is do you know how you want it lettered, that's the question. Do you want block or script? Sans-serif or serif? Gold leaf or paint? Shadowed or plain?"

He talked a good game and he turned out to be as good as his word. Working in my little dinghy, he sketched an outline of the letters on the transom in pencil, freehand without even using a ruler, then asked me if that was what I wanted. I said it looked fine. He then painted *"Visitor IV"* in letters ten inches high in that same deep blue and outlined them in red. Christ, it was beautiful! He went on to redo my mahogany name boards in gold lettering with black trim. He disappeared after I paid him and I never saw him again. I often wondered where he had learned his craft and how he had made a living at it in a place like St. Lucia. There weren't many yacht transoms in the harbor.

It hit me one day that I could no longer live with the chaos of wires in the engine room. I had been trying to trace through a wire and had gotten nowhere. I called Ramshen and we had a council of war.

"Look, Ramshen," I said with the two of us hunched down in the engine room," I'm going to start by tracing out a wire. If it doesn't do anything, I want you to pull it out. Take all the cable clamps, staples, screws and anything else that comes with it. While you're working on that one, I'll be tracing out the next one. And we aren't going to quit until I know what every wire is doing, if anything."

We traced and pulled for three days. When we were finished, Ramshen had two bushelbaskets packed full of wires. Some we salvaged for possible future use. Most we threw out. It was one of the most satisfying jobs I did on *Visitor*. While we were at it, I pulled the ancient Tungar battery charger which, although I respected it for what it had accomplished for 30 years, had to go. There was a new rectifier unit in the locker and it was time it went to work.

Keeping batteries charged was critical on *Visitor*. Someone had long ago removed the generators from the engines, probably because the huge and complicated voltage regulators were difficult to get serviced in remote places like St. Lucia. We relied on 110-volt shore power or the 3 kw. diesel generator to drive the battery charger and kept a constant eye on the charge by reading the battery volt meter every day or so. I put in a charge about once a week. How I would have liked to have had an automatic charger, but the cost would have been prohibitive.

Having come this far and feeling good about our success in the engine room, I decided to go after the plumbing as well. Ramshen and I used the same system that we had used with the wires and it worked just as well.

I found the most astonishing rat's nest of valves. There were seven in all, clamped to an old board which was nailed, yes, nailed in place to the floorboards in a completely inaccessible corner of the engine room. Some valves were connected to short bits of hose, some to pipe. All were interconnected in some way or another, but none of the hoses or pipes were connected to anything else. I think it must have been part of some hairbrained system for changing over the fresh water from shore to the on board tanks. Whatever it was, I consigned it to the trash heap with a sigh of relief. I was grateful that none of my friends had seen it and asked me what it did.

Having eliminated the useless piping, I set about putting to order that which was useful. There were five pumps in the engine room and they were scattered everywhere that was inaccessible. One at a time, I removed them from the boat and cleaned and rebuilt them on the locker's workbench, installing valves, gaskets, packing, impellers and the like, as required. I reinstalled them all, the fresh water pump, the shower drain pump, the bilge pump, the air conditioning salt water cooling pump and the electric head pump, in a row on a new, sturdy wooden platform that could be easiliy reached. Then I ran new wires and new piping to them. When that was finished, I painted them all white.

It's a funny thing about those pumps, all sitting there in a row, looking new and business-like. I don't think anyone ever saw them there but me. They still did the same jobs they had done before I changed them around. The only difference was that now I knew them on a first-name basis and I knew that they were installed properly. It was a lot of work in a cramped and hot space. At times, I cursed a pipe that lay in too short or a wire that was dead and should have been hot. I cursed the sweat that ran down into my eyes so that I couldn't see. Like all mechanics, I skinned knuckles, cut fingers, ripped fingernails and cursed again. But when it was done, the white paint dry and the little brass nameplate I had found on the bilge pump cleaned of layers of paint, shined up and reinstalled with new brass screws—when it was all completed, I sat there in the engine room and looked at them, just looked at them for an hour. Later that night, I woke up and went back and looked at them again. I was always happy to think about them, and had there been anyone who would have understood how well they looked, I would have been happy to show them off. But there wasn't and that was all right with me. I knew they were there.

By now, I had about had it with engine rooms. I felt that I had been reduced in stature by at least a foot from so much work in a crouching position. My knees had oil permanently embedded in the skin and my hands would have made a good "before" photo for one of those hand cream ads. Ramshen had obviously had enough of it too, for he was not quite the willing worker these days he had once been. In fact, I was beginning to worry about him. And my next project didn't help matters much. I decided it was time we did something about the wheelhouse. I had made a few exploratory experiments with varnish remover and I knew that under all those thick layers of age-blackened varnish there lay some beautiful mahogany.

Ramshen and I had a long talk about the dangers of using varnish remover. I made him practice how to flush his eyes with water from a hose in case he splashed the remover on his face. I explained that there was no hurry about the job; that it would take a long time and that it would be boring, tedious work; and that I would break it up for him with other jobs as often as possible. I wanted the whole thing taken down to bare wood, filled and stained and given three coats of flat polyurethane varnish.

It took about a week for Ramshen to understand what I had been talking about. After a while, I think he realized that I had meant everything I had said, especially about going slowly and doing it right. One of Ramshen's really sterling qualities was that he could learn to do most anything. His only problem, one common to many young people, was his attitude. He could do anything he *wanted* to do.

While he was learning the ropes of varnish work, I did odd jobs in the area of the wheelhouse so that I could keep an eye on his progress. I didn't want the wood damaged by carelessness or because I had failed to show him how to do something well enough. I installed a rudder angle indicator, something I have always considered important on a twin-engine boat. I ripped out and pitched into the water, ecology not withstanding, a horrible, house-type wall light fixture that was supposed to serve as a chart light and replaced it with a proper marine chart light.

The starter buttons for the main engines were actually automotive headlight dimmer switches, no doubt all some poor soul could find when the originals had needed replacement. I couldn't stand the sight of them. Don Phipps, my good friend and fellow boating enthusiast in Boston, had sent me two beautiful Cutler Hammer start button assemblies with red buttons and aluminum "start" nameplates. Somehow, the old 6-71s seemed to roll over with more authority after those babies were installed.

My mother had come down in the midst of all this chaotic work to see what her wayward son was up to and had stayed on board for a week. We had both had a fine visit. When she was leaving, she had asked me what I wanted for Christmas, and I knew exactly what I wanted: a new digital fathometer. Bless her heart, she gave it to me; that is to say, I ordered it because she had no more idea of what a digital fathometer was than she could fly a jet plane, and she paid for it. I installed it in the wheelhouse while Ramshen continued scraping up gooey varnish remover.

Actually, I had a bit of luck installing the depth sounder's transducer. I had checked out the existing one underneath the hull with scuba gear and had concluded that the old fairing block would do just fine. The through hull part of the new transducer was the same diameter as the old. I coated the connector end of the new transducer cable with silicone grease, then wrapped it with plastic and taped the whole mess. Next, I took Ramshen off his varnish work and down into the engine room and showed him where the old transducer was. I told him to wait until I had gotten in the water and had tapped on the hull from below. He was then to undo the retaining nut and tap out the old unit, while I removed the one wood screw which held the old unit from the underwater side. I showed him the wire that I would push up from below, and how to place the new washer and retaining nut on the wire. After that, he should gently pull the wire, ignoring what little bit of water might come in, until the shaft of the new unit came through. He was then to thread up the nut as tightly as he could by hand.

I had gotten a dab of underwater epoxy compound out of Ross, so I coated the hull side of the new transducer with it. The whole job took four minutes and came off like clockwork. Never let it be said you have to haul a boat to put in a new transducer.

It took Ramshen a month, broken up by occasional odd jobs and a few day charters, to get the wheelhouse stripped, filled, stained and coated once with varnish. I did the last two coats because, as good as he was, I was still a better hand with a varnish brush than Ramshen. I had also taken down the steering wheel, which had turned out to be a lovely old thing inlaid with a different color of wood. I refinished it in gloss polyurethane. The decking in the wheelhouse had been perfectly serviceable teak, but it was hard to keep it looking right with all the charterers dirtying it up with their street shoes, so I covered it with deep blue, foam-backed carpet tiles as a finishing touch.

About this time, I was notified that my new carpeting for the salon had arrived from England and was in customs. Many arduous and bitter experiences had taught me not to try to clear anything through customs myself. International yachts, those which left the island at least several times a year and had not permanently entered the state, nor been assessed for customs duty, were not liable for import duty on items clearly intended for use on board. It was merely necessary for a customs inspector to see the goods delivered aboard. For some reason, clerks in the customs office seemed to take this as a personal affront and could put a yachtsman through the tortures of the damned. Forms of incredible complexity would often be filled out in painful detail, then not be examined and passed upon for days at a time. More often than not, they were simply "lost". A small error in filling out a form would cause it to be rejected and returned without an indication of what the error was. "De form does be wrong, man," was the most help one could expect. Once, for example, I had entered a weight in pounds rather than hundredweight. Correcting that took four days and five return trips to the customs office, often waiting in line for more than an hour each time.

The answer to the problem was to hire a broker, who would, for some reason, not be subject to the harassment. Of course, brokers charged fat fees, far out of proportion to what they actually did, but for the belligerence, antagonism and rudeness which they enabled yachtsmen to avoid, it was worth it.

And so I called the broker I had been using and, two days later, my new orange carpet arrived. I spread it out on the fuel dock, having had Ramshen do a good job of sweeping the dock first. I laid it out pile down and then, using the old indoor-outdoor carpet as a template, marked out the shape and dimensions with a felt pen. It took only minutes to cut it out and, before long, it had been laid on the floorboards of the salon and the newly reupholstered furniture had been moved into place.

For me, this was a turning point. I could see the light at the end of the tunnel for the first time. There were still many, many things to be done. But somehow, when that carpet went down, I felt as though I had really begun to accomplish something with *Visitor IV*. She was my home. She was beautiful. She was something to be proud of. I was really pleased.

I went on to redo the varnish on the teak paneling in the salon with a matte finish and uncovered some painted-over mahogany trim in the two staterooms. I even painted the engine room white and cut up the old salon indoor-outdoor carpeting and laid it on the engine room floorboards. I spent almost two weeks rebuilding some questionable flooring in the crew's quarters and the shower floor as well. Another major project was to remove the life rail stanchions, including the mahogany rail cap. Many of the screws holding the stanchions to the deck were pulling loose and the only remedy was to drill out all the old screw holes and glue in wood dowels. Then the whole thing had to be put together again. It was a long, tedious job.

Work on the boat really stopped at that point. My first charter season was upon me and I was too busy with it to do any work except for routine maintenance and necessary repairs.

Later on, during the next off season, I went back to it again. The first job at that point was to get *Visitor* hauled and her bottom scraped and painted. Fortunately, St. Lucia still had her excellent marine railway then. Shortly after *Visitor* was hauled, the railway was abandoned because of a massive harbor dredging project which called for filling in the area where it was located.

I was apprehensive about hauling *Visitor*. She had been recently surveyed when I bought her and so I had not had one done at that time. This was to be the first chance I had had to see her really out of the water. When she was hauled, scraped

70

off and dry, I went over her bottom and transom with Malcolm Gardner-Hobbs, who was the manager of the slipway as well as the Lloyd's representative in St. Lucia. We also had the slipway's very able shipwright, Bonnie Williamson, with us. We found a damaged spot in the wood around the port exhaust pipe where it came through the transom, and one soft butt joint, not bad for a 30-year-old boat which hadn't been out of tropical water in more than 18 months. Bonnie went after the soft wood with a vengence. There is real joy in watching a man skilled with wood. He chiseled out what seemed to me to be tremendous holes in the two bad spots, and chamfered the edges. He then cut new pieces from scrap mahogany as carefully as if they were pieces for a priceless antique. He fitted them into place with a polysulfide sealant and screwed everything together with battens on the inside. When the screw holes were bunged and everything was sanded and primed, you would have never known anything had been wrong.

Visitor's bottom had been done in the past with Petit's unepoxy and I used it again, selecting their light blue color. We did the boot top with the same dark navy blue that had been used for *Visitor*'s trim. When she splashed back into the water, she looked better than ever.

The only bad thing that happened during hauling was that I had had to can Ramshen. We had had several long talks about his attitude, and I had tried to tell him that while I could put up with a lot, the charterers were not to have to put up with anything. We had had a real showdown once when he had refused to do something a charterer had asked him to do, and I had told him that one more bit of trouble would mean his job. Looking back, I think he had had enough of *Visitor* and wanted a change.

I had told him that every day we spent on the slipway was costing us a lot of money, and that I expected him to keep busy with scraping and painting so that we could get off as quickly as possible. When I had found him goofing off and keeping the other men I had hired to help with the job from getting their work done, I had paid him two weeks' wages and given him his walking papers. It hadn't been an easy thing to

71

do. He had been my first crewman and I had developed a genuine liking for him. We had done a lot of work together, and I would never forget that dark, rainy night in Kingstown Harbor when he had told me to "Pull, goddamnit!"

I guess the grapevine worked fairly well in St. Lucia, because the day after I had let Ramshen go, young men began to come around looking for his old job. I had to turn many of them away because they either couldn't speak English well enough to work with the charterers, or because they didn't show the neatness and manners that I felt were required. A couple of days went by like this and then Raymond showed up. Raymond looked as though he were part East Indian and part black. He was a good-looking kid, neat in appearance and almost shy. I was ready to hire him on the spot, but I asked him if he had any experience with boats.

"No, Mr. Bob," he said.

"Well," I asked, "why do you want to work on *Visitor IV?*"

"I need a job," he replied.

I told him to start in the morning. That kind of honesty I respect. But Raymond didn't work out and it was a damn shame. He tried. Oh, how he tried. But he just couldn't learn. Everything I told him went in one ear and out the other. Show him how to hold a paintbrush on Monday morning and you could count on having to do it all over again if you wanted any painting done on Tuesday. He was willing. He was polite. But he just couldn't learn.

At one point I thought he would make a raving maniac out of me. For three weeks, I had wanted to get some varnishing done outside. And for three weeks it had rained or threatened to rain. Every morning I would say to Raymond, "Looks like another rainy day, Raymond. We won't be able to varnish today," and I would give him something else to work on. Then one day it broke. The sun came up all bright and cheery, the sky was Caribbean blue and I said, "Today, Raymond, we can varnish." I spent two hours with him showing him how to sand lightly and clean thoroughly, then brush on a light coat of varnish. Actually, he seemed to have picked it up fairly

72

well. I had things to do in town that morning and so I left him with the life rail caps and window trim to work on. I thought he would be done by midafternoon, so I had lunch in town and got back to Ganter's about three o'clock. I had the feeling as I walked toward *Visitor*'s dock that I had been away too long. I was right.

There was Raymond, standing on top of the wheelhouse with a bucket of soapy water in one hand and the water hose in the other. Having finished with the varnishing and having nothing else to do, he had taken it into his head to wash the boat, one of his regular chores. I had the cleanest wet varnish in town. Raymond had to go.

It would have been nice if I had owned *Visitor IV* outright. Unfortunately, I didn't. The bank owned her. But we had an agreement whereby, in return for a substantial amount of money to be sent to it each month, I could play with *Visitor* all I wanted to. It had seemed like a good idea at the time. She was involved in an "established day charter business," and all I had to do was stand there on the dock and let the passengers walk aboard, money clutched in their hot little hands. Yah. Unhuh.

About midway through the first season, I went down to Beverly's office and asked her where all the damn charterers were. Oh, I had had business, and a fair amount of it, but nowhere near enough to keep the bank happy. Beverly said that it looked like it would be a bad season. A lot of our tourists came from Canada, and that country was embroiled in an air controller's strike. The economy was going to the dogs everywhere. And besides, no one had ever known whether Monty had really made any significant money with *Visitor IV*. He had never been willing to divulge what his earnings had been,

I suppose for fear of getting caught in some kind of tax bind.

At the end of seven months, the end of my first season, I was broke. My bills were paid, but, the way things were going, and with only the off season of six or seven months to look forward to, I knew I was in trouble. In desperation, I wrote to my bank and told them I just couldn't keep up the payment level I had agreed to. Could my payment be cut in half, I asked. Never let it be said all bankers are bums. They wrote back agreeing to my request. With that lucky break, I knew I could make ends meet.

I took my day chartering seriously and I hope that that helped to account for what little success I had at it. The biggest problem was to get people to go. Impossible as it seemed to a boat owner, there were people in this world who just didn't like boats. It was a hard thing for me to accept. But I did get charters and in many different ways. Beverly had her reputation as a charter agent well established on the island, and she provided me with probably about 15 percent of my business, in return for a 10 percent commission, of course. As time went by, I developed certain benefactors among the staff of the hotels. Some were as devoted to me and my fledgling business as a mother to her child.

David Stephenson was such an individual. He was manager of one of the largest and newest hotels on the Island and a bit of a wild Cornishman. I had a phone on the boat which was indispensable for my business. He would quite often call me late Friday night and say, "Are you going out tomorrow?" Saturdays were slow days and he knew perfectly well I was not.

"Fine," he would say, "ring you right back!"

David would then simply mingle among the hotel guests, as I had often seen him do when I was at the hotel in the evening, spot a likely couple and say to them, "Tomorrow you are going to have the best day of your stay here. You are going out for a day on the Yacht *Visitor IV*. It'll cost you twenty dollars U.S. each, and you're to be in the lobby, ready to go, at eight-thirty sharp." And because David was David, they would go.

He was really doing his guests a service for there was little to do in St. Lucia, and those activities that were available were poorly promoted. Most hotels would not allow me to advertise openly because they felt it would take business away from their water sports concessionaires who offered water-skiing, snorkeling and small sailboats from the hotel's beach. David's hotel was so new, however, that they didn't have a water sports operation. He quite often rounded up groups as large as twenty, and the only thing he ever asked in return was to be allowed to go himself at no cost. In fact, I shouldn't say that. He never asked. I had told him and the staff of all the hotels that they could take their days off on *Visitor* at no charge, anytime she was going on a trip. Obviously, it was good advertising. It didn't cost me anything as the boat was going anyway, and we were never full to capacity unless we had a special group. Groups were another source of business. They deserve to be mentioned, and not much else.

The other method of getting business was to hustle, and I hated it. I was too much of a New Englander. After all, we were born and raised on the philosophy that one didn't speak to strangers unless properly introduced. Nothing could be more abhorrent than bending the arm and ear of someone you didn't know and quite possibly would prefer not to know.

Actually, it had its good moments and its bad. It consisted of getting dressed up in my striped slacks, dark blue turtleneck and white dinner jacket and making the rounds of the hotels during cocktail hour. I, like David Stephenson, would seek out a likely prospect and try to engage him or her in small talk. This could be easily worked around to *Visitor* because there was so little to do on St. Lucia that "what to do" was a major topic of conversation. At that point, I would give a brief sales pitch, press one of my brochures in their hands and be off for a new victim. To this approach, I got reactions which ranged from, "Look, fella, don't bother me with that crap," to firm bookings for the next day from the people I had been talking to and the five or six other couples they had made friends with during their stay in St. Lucia.

But I still didn't like hustling. It was easiest when there had been a large group from one hotel aboard *Visitor* that day. I would appear at their hotel cocktail hour that evening and be greeted like a conquering hero by my customers, because people really did have the time of their lives on *Visitor*. All the backslapping and the "Hi, Captain!" and the "What a day we had on your boat" hoorah would draw a crowd of people to whom I would be required to explain what all the excitement had been about. Pressed on to fill in glossed-over details of the day's trip by happy customers, I always walked away with a boatload signed up for the next day. That was the way I liked to do it. I felt as though I had been introduced by my friends. And I guess quite often I had.

A day with a scheduled charter began early. I was up at the crack of dawn every morning in St. Lucia. I was living that kind of life, then. The days were good ones and I was always anxious to get to them. The first job was to make enough rum punch to meet the needs of the number of people that would be coming that day. In the early days when I needed the money, I went with as few as four charterers but, by the second season, I put my minimum at ten. Even that was not always adhered to.

Making rum punch is an art. No two people make it the same way or with the same ingredients. And everyone, myself included, keeps their recipe a secret. I did admit publicly to using St. Lucian honey and guava juice from Trinidad along with other things. Mt. Gay Rum was too good (and too expensive) to dilute with all that glop. I used a Barbadian rum and made a rum punch that could hold its head up in any company. It was served, free, all day by my crewman, who grated fresh nutmeg on the top of each glassful and, as a final touch, floated a bougainvillaea blossom on each. I had made a special mahogany serving tray for him with holes that held 15 glasses in place as he maneuvered around the decks while we were under way. He looked damn smart in his white knit tee shirt, white shorts and sneakers as he served those superb drinks to delighted guests.

I always thought the greatest testimonial to my rum punch

78

was that, in spite of hundreds, possibly thousands, of gallons of the stuff that I had made, I still liked to drink it myself. Quite often, I enjoyed a leftover glass at the end of the day.

We always got under way at nine o'clock, so I wanted my crewman aboard at eight. This gave him time to vacuum the carpeting, clean up the galley, wipe down the boat outside, set out the bow cushions and deck chairs and get changed into his charter clothes. I was left free to check out the engines, fuel, water, the heads and answer the phone to get last minute reservations, or phone around to locate latecomers. I was also on hand to greet each of the guests as they came aboard. It was often the busiest hour of the day.

The guests had to get from their hotels to the boat on their own. Most came by taxi, but if there were a large group from one hotel, the hotel bus would often bring them. The little parking lot at Ganter's was right in front of *Visitor's* dock. On good days, when it would fill up and taxis and busses would create a minor traffic jam, I would take pride in my little business. It didn't happen nearly often enough, however.

My charterers came in all sizes, shapes, colors and creeds. They came from virtually every country in the world; I even had a Russian couple on board one day. And they were of every disposition from saccharine sweet to Texas tough. Some were generous and some tight as a tick. Some minded their own business and enjoyed their day. Others minded my business and ruined my day. After a while, it seemed as though there were some certain types that I could always count on to be in any large group. I got so that I could spot them, even as they came aboard.

The worst of the lot was the stereotyped American tourist. He was overfed and underbrained. He wore Bermuda shorts, street shoes, a flowery Hawaiian shirt and a straw hat. He smoked a cigar, dropped his ashes on the carpet and ground the butt into the deck. He greeted me with "Hi there, Captain!" in a voice that would blister the brightwork and was all smiles and geniality until he had to be told, "That rum punch crap is *all* there is aboard," and "No, I don't have any

79

Scotch." From then on, he sulked and nothing would please him for the rest of the day. He would pay me without a word when we got back and leave, mumbling, "I'll talk to the hotel manager about this crap." I hated to see him come and was glad to see him go. Fortunately, there weren't many of his kind, but, when he showed up, it took 20 pleasant charterers to get him out of my mind. His wife always seemed to be a nonentity, having probably been beaten into submission by years of living with him. She said little and did less during the day.

The vast majority were my kind of people. They came with their cameras and suntan lotion, with good spirits and a "let's have a good time" attitude, and that's what they got. Most were couples, most were middle-aged, most were of above average income and well-educated. They were about 30 percent British, 30 percent Canadian and 30 percent American. The rest were a mixed bag, ranging from the occasional West Indian tourist to the Russian couple I mentioned before. Of the lot, I liked the Canadians the best. They were out to have a good time and that's what it was all about. And they could afford my price of U.S. $20 per person. The Americans had traveled too much and were too loud and too demanding. The British couldn't afford to be doing what they were doing and so were afraid to enjoy themselves. A week or two in St.Lucia was an expensive trip for anyone, but especially the British. They just didn't have the money.

There were a few spinsters in pairs; a few young couples on honeymoons, blessed by clergy or not; even gay couples. You name 'em, I've had 'em on *Visitor IV*. Yet with all the variety, I don't think there ever was anyone who was really openly offensive to me or the other guests. There was never a real troublemaker. Those who chose to get their money's worth out of the free rum punch could usually hold it. The loudmouths were compensated for by the quiet ones. Those who found *Visitor* to be not what they had expected were offset by those who found the day to be much more than they had hoped for.

The biggest problem for me was the wearing effect of the hundreds of well-meaning but still thoughtless people who fired questions broadside at me all day long. In the first place, the questions were always the same:

How long is the boat?

How much does she draw, Captain?

How fast does she go?

How long will it take to get there?

What are the . . . ah . . . locals like?

Are there any sharks?

How long have you lived here?

Do you like it here?

Don't you get lonely?

How much is the boat worth?

How much do you make at this?

You ever think about selling?

And the prize, from one of the American Tourist types, with his cigar in his mouth and his elbow in my ribs: "What are you doing for tail, Captain? Banging the natives?"

And in the second place, I was busy. I was steering the boat and keeping an eye on the water ahead for fish pot floats. These were made of about three feet of green bamboo and lay in the troughs of the little six to twelve inch waves, just waiting to get into my props. I would be wondering why I hadn't seen my crewman in the past five minutes. I would be wondering why the port engine was running a bit hotter than usual. I would be wondering if the taxis would be at the jetty in Soufriere when we got there. And a hundred other things. I will never forget one clown who, while I was docking at the cement jetty in Soufriere with a three foot swell coming into the beach, wanted to know what time it was. He was incensed when I wouldn't take my eyes off the cement, which was 12 inches from my pitching hull, to look at my watch.

The problem was that the wheelhouse was fairly large, comfortable and the best place to look at the view while under way. And people like to talk to the "Captain." I never had the heart to close it off. I could have; there were separate doors to every access. But I never did.

Quite often, the men would be envious of what I was doing. They would say, "Exactly what I want to do, but I just haven't got the guts." I never felt very sorry for them. If they had guts enough to survive in the business world, they could easily have done what I did.

When the questions got too bad, I would turn the squelch down on the marine radio and, if necessary, the volume up. I remember one dear lady, undaunted by the radio, asked, "Captain, do you always have that radio so loud?"

"No'm," I replied in mock seriousness, "just today."

She didn't get it and went on with her questions.

There was another day when automatically throwing back the same answers got me in a bind. Some well-meaning soul started her question, "Captain, how long . . ." Thinking she was going to ask how long I had been in St. Lucia, I interrupted her. "About two years, ma'am." A moment's silence followed and then a quiet, tiny voice said, "Oh, I was going to ask how long the boat was." I turned to look at her, but it was too late. She was crestfallen.

But there were others I didn't feel so bad about crushing. I remember one scrawny, rather mean-looking woman with a big nose and a Brooklyn accent, decked out in an Hawaiian muumuu and an absurd hat, who breezed aboard saying, "Oh, my dears. Isn't it all just too, too? I mean don't you just love it? But surely, Captain, you don't *live* here." At that point, my friend of about a year made his appearance by coming up the galley steps. Sam was the finest Siamese cat I had ever seen. He had been given to me by Beverly.

"Oh, my God!" exclaimed bigmouth in a voice that all could hear. "I can't stand cats!"

In one of those strokes of conversational genuis which come to me all too infrequently in life, I put my head very close to hers and, in the dead silence that had followed her thoughtless remark, said very quietly and in my most confidential tone, "That's all right, madam. Sam doesn't like people." she left *Visitor* then and there with the laughter of about twenty people ringing in her ears. It was the best twenty dollars I ever lost.

When all the noses had been counted and I had every one that was expected, I would give the crewman a high sign and he would disconnect the telephone and shore power cables while I fired up the engines. The crewman would take the lines in, one at a time, on a signal from me in the wheelhouse and, when we were all clear, I'd back her out with a long blast on the horn. *Visitor* had manual shifts and you could lift yourself right off the wheelhouse deck pulling them into reverse, if you didn't know how it was done. For one thing, you did them one at a time, bracing yourself against the lever you weren't trying to engage. You also did it smartly and with both feet firmly planted on the deck. I got used to it and, besides, it looked impressive as hell to the guests. A port and starboard twist off the end of the dock and we were clear to head up Vigie Creek into the Harbor. There were usually a few cruising yachts at anchor, and a good tale could be told about at least one of them. Most were live-aboards and, often, very small children were playing quietly on deck. They would look up and wave at the delighted guests. From Castries, we turned south to head down the lee coast of St. Lucia.

My brochure told it in a nutshell:

Day cruises out of Castries Harbor pass Morne Fortune and Vigie Hill, the scenes of countless battles between the British and French.

Heading south down the leeward coast, *Visitor* passes lush green hills, palm and banana trees growing down to the water's edge, beaches of golden sand, small fishing villages and picturesque bays.

Arriving at Soufriere Town, *Visitor* will tie up for several hours. Here guests may shop, lunch or walk around the church square where in 1785, a guillotine was set up to bring the benefits of the French Revolution to St. Lucia.

You may want to hire a taxi to drive up the old French road to the Botanical Garden or the bubbling sulfurous springs which once soothed the weary 18th century warriors of Louis XVI. Here too is the famous drive-in volcano where you can safely walk in a crater through which sulfur steam still escapes.

Leaving Soufriere Harbor, guests will find a breath taking view (don't forget your camera) of the world famous Pitons—twin volcanic spires towering above the ocean. A mariner's landmark for centuries, these dramatic lava cones create a cathedral-like aura as *Visitor* quietly passes through Anse des Pitons.

Returning north to Castries, *Visitor* will stop for swimming (don't forget suit and towel!) and visit Marigot Bay where British men-of-war once hid from prying French eyes. Perhaps the most beautiful anchorage in the West Indies, Marigot Bay was recently the backdrop for the American film, *Dr. Dolittle.*

A little schmaltzy, perhaps, but not bad as travel/tourist brochures go. I've read stuff that was so syrupy that you had to wash your hands after putting it down. And besides, mine told the truth. The hills really are lush and green and the palms and banana trees really do come down to the water's edge. The guillotine I only have history's word for, however. The *Dr. Dolittle* filming was ancient history even then, but people remembered it and were delighted to see Marigot Bay.

My biggest challenge of the day was the jetty at Soufriere. The outside edge of this cement monstrosity was exactly six inches above my sheer in calm water which meant that, with exceptionally fat fenders, I could just barely keep my rail stanchions from taking the load as we came alongside. The bow was raised and flared, and any good fender would protect that part of *Visitor.* The problem was that, about a third of the time, there was a swell at the jetty that ran from one foot on good days to three feet on rough days. Perhaps four times a season it would be bad enough to prevent me from coming alongside at all. I had had to develop some remarkable skill in approaching that jetty and I knew every inch of its extended edge. There were certain places, for example, where fragments of what had once been a wooden facing of 12" by 12" greenheart beams remained, projecting under and beyond the outside edge. If I could stop *Visitor* just off those beams and get a line to the jetty to work on, then my fenders would rest safely there, even in the swell. Of course, I had to be careful not to puncture a fender on a retaining bolt which projected from the wood at one point.

There were no cleats on the jetty, only very small steel rings embedded in the cement. My line handlers ashore were the small boys who hung around the jetty, and they knew nothing about tying knots that I could reliably work against with two 200-horsepower engines. By pure luck, I had found three large, galvanized sister hooks, fitted with thimbles, at a store in town. I had Cracker splice them to 15-foot lengths of 3/4" nylon and I used them as docking lines. The boys saw how the sister hooks worked and, once they were on the rings, I could do anything. Of course, that was later on, in the days when the boys would help, willingly.

The first few times I came into Soufriere, the boys were hell on wheels. To start with, they refused to help with the lines and my crewman had to do some fancy foot work. When we were tied up and my guests began to disembark, these little brown darlings, many without clothes because they were in the water as much as they were out of it, began to urinate where they stood. That completed, they would taunt the guests with what few English obscenities and all the patois ones they knew, and they knew enough to get by. When a guest would try to take a photograph of one of them, he would immediately turn around and bend over, showing that part of his anatomy which he wanted photographed for the folks back home.

It got so bad that I had to ask the Soufriere Police to intervene, but it was the local police who told me what the problem was. Of course, I was making basically the same run that Monty Robinson had made and *Visitor* was well known to the boys. It was known as the boat that belonged to that rich white man who was too cheap to give a quarter to a little dock boy who might help with the lines. They hated his guts and rightly so. The fact that a different white man was running the boat meant nothing to them. Being both white and "rich" in their eyes, I could be counted on to give them the same treatment.

It took time. I began by inviting every police officer who came down to the dock aboard for a tour of the boat. None of

85

them had ever been invited inside before. Eventually, one youngster, who was a little too young to understand the hate or had perhaps not been around long enough to know the cause of it, began to stop and talk with me while the guests were touring Soufriere. In time, I got him to agree to take the lines. He took a lot of criticism from his chums but he also always got a quarter from my crewman. I thought it would be better if he gave the money to the boy rather than I, and I kept a supply of quarters in the wheelhouse for the purpose.

After that it was all downhill. The kids would fight to see who would take the lines and often several quarters had to be dispensed. It was money well spent. The boys became little gentlemen, often helping older people off the boat and offering to show them where to buy things. I taught them to dive into the water to catch coins thrown by the guests. Although I was criticized for it by some of the parents as demeaning the children, I didn't buy a word of it. Kids in places all over the world do it where, as in Soufriere, it is the only way most of them can get spending money. More than that, they got good at it and caught almost all the coins. Each child would pop to the surface, his face lit up with pleasure after a successful dive. He would put the coin in his mouth, shriek with joy, and then clobber the boys next to him as he tried to catch another. It was great fun for everyone. The guests took movies and snapshots and came away thinking what great kids they were. And indeed they were good kids, given a fair crack at a little piece of the pie.

The kids were a big help to me in another way. Once, when I was making my usual approach, they waved me off. They were always clowning around, so I didn't pay any attention. By then, it was too late. I realized the boat was headed sideways for the end corner of the jetty and was completely out of control. I couldn't imagine what was pushing me sideways. We hit with a sickening crunch which cracked some topside planking. I had gotten into trouble because, once or twice a year, there was a freak current of four or five knots which went parallel to the shore and at a right angle to the jetty. It had caught me broadside. I backed clear and, after assessing the situation and understanding what had happened, I came around again, bow on against the current, and tied up easily across the end of the jetty. From that day on, I never failed to look at the water around the pilings for telltale signs of current. And when the kids tried to wave me off, I looked for the reason.

Once the boat was tied up, the next job was to get everyone aboard taxis for the trip to see the sulfur springs and the old mineral baths in the hills behind the town of Soufriere. It was a rugged half-hour ride to see these questionable sights, and I often felt a little guilty about recommending them. Interesting, perhaps, to a few, but not much more. The springs lay in a moonscape-like area of about two or three acres where sulfurous vapors rose from subterranean caldrons that attested to the island's volcanic origins. It was hot, smelly and difficult to get around in. But small children sold brilliantly yellow samples of sulfur crystals for "small change", and it really was possible to walk in a volcano's crater.

The nearby mineral baths were a historical nothing, but the road to them went through magnificent foliage. A trip along it offered tourists a chance to see a towering rain forest with bamboo and giant ferns; banana, breadfruit and cacao trees; and vanilla plants, to say nothing of too many varieties of flowers to mention by name.

The taxis returned to the guesthouse of dear and gracious Mrs. Allain where my charterers would be treated to their only chance to have a real West Indian dinner. Many were skeptical as they were guided up the narrow wooden stairs to the guesthouse dining room over the Allain's general store, which was run by son Chiko. Mr. Allain was usually busy with his nearby plantation.

The dining room was set family style with four long tables placed end to end. It was capable of seating about twenty-five. No two glasses were the same and the eating utensils were similarly disparate. Dime store plastic doilies were at each place, but there were real flowers, cut that morning, gracing every table. The wood floor was covered in places with lino-

87

leum, in other places only with wear. The chairs were also vintage dime store with plastic backs and seats on chrome frames. But none of this really mattered. Mrs. Allain was a cook and an excellent one. My doubting guests had to be coaxed to sit down. They called for a lot of drinks after the hot drive in the country.

Eventually, Mrs. Allain's daughters began to bring out the first course: West Indian pumpkin soup. Delicious beyond belief, hot, spicey and flavorful, it eliminated the skepticism. Then the meal began. For nearly half an hour, the girls made nonstop trips to the kitchen where Mrs. Allain heaped platters with her West Indian specialties. The platters were simply put on the tables and it was boardinghouse formality from there on. She varied the menu depending on the availability of food, but she always had Creole chicken, superb, deep-fried breadfruit balls (the only way to eat that otherwise tasteless stuff), pan-fried flying fish or dolphin, deep-fried salt fish cakes, fried plantain (a kind of cooking banana), rice covered with a vegetable sauce, kidney beans, sweet potatoes (yams) and a green salad. Dessert was always a choice of either fruit from their plantation or their homemade guava ice cream. Everything was on an "eat all you want" basis, and for this, Mrs. Allain charged the equivalent of a little less than three dollars per person.

How they loved it. "This is what we wanted," they would say. "All we get at the hotel is steak. Hell, we can get that anywhere!"

By now, my gang was full, tired and pleased. They would reboard *Visitor* and we would take a slow cruise about a mile farther south to Anse des Pitons or, the bay of the pitons. This beautiful little spot gave the guests a close-up view of the pitons which they could not get from shore. I used to anchor there for swimming because it was so beautiful, until one day when I had a near disaster.

It was one of those travel brochure days: blue, cloudless sky, and mild, warm breeze. We were on anchor with the swimming ladder over and about eight or ten swimmers were in the water. There was a magnificent Dutch motor yacht of about 110 feet anchored with us. I was below in the galley, making up some more rum punch, when I heard the wind begin to blow. Knowing the anchoring was poor, I started up to the wheelhouse to have a look. By the time I got there, the wind was blowing 20 knots off shore. I called for my crewman and he came to the wheelhouse door. I told him to get the swimming ladder in and to get up on the bow in case we had to up anchor. *Visitor* had excellent all-around visibility from her wheelhouse and I could see that there were no swimmers in the water. They were all on the beach and it was a damn good thing they were. It took my crewman about a minute to get the ladder in, but by the time he got to the bow and the anchor line, it was blowing so hard that had he let go of the line, he would have been blown off the boat. I estimated the wind at 40 to 50 knots. We were dragging anchor. I looked for the Dutch yacht and was shocked to see about ten inches of her bottom paint showing on her windward side. The skipper, trying to free his anchor, had worked around broadside to the wind, and the wind was blowing him over about 10 or 15 degrees. That was the last time I saw him. Just as quickly as the wind had come up, it started to rain and visibility dropped to 50 feet in 60 seconds. I could just make out my crewman on the bow, still hanging on for dear life to that anchor line.

While all this was going on, I started *Visitor's* faithful engines. Because of the way the wind was blowing me, I had to come around into it in order to turn again and head out of the bay to sea. When the rain started, I made a quick note of the compass course I would need to apply to get out. I put the rudder over full and went ahead full on one engine and back full on the other. We just sat there. In fact, the compass told me we were losing against the wind. I couldn't swing the bow into it, even with the full force of two 200-horsepower engines.

The only alternative was to reverse everything and try to back away from it. This worked, although I was going sideways more than reverse. At least I got some maneuvering room between me and the shore. Finally, I got my stern to the wind, found my compass course and, using just enough power to maintain steerage, I headed out to sea. I was frightened to death of colliding with the other yacht. I had no idea where she was, and we were both operating all over a small bay trying to get to the same place: out. While she no doubt had radar, she certainly didn't have it on that day. As it turned out, the whole emergency was over by the time it would have taken radar to warm up.

Five minutes later, the weather had passed me and was out to sea. The Dutch yacht was nowhere in sight. I headed back in to pick up my frightened, but safe charterers as my crewman began taking in the anchor line, which by now was hanging free in more than 500 feet of water. It was that deep, close to the shore of this volcanic island. The charterers had found shelter in the lee of the ruins of an old sugar refinery which stood near the shore.

When we got back to Ganter's that afternoon, the Dutch yacht was tied up at the fuel dock and I went over to compare notes with the skipper. His beautifully equipped wheelhouse had a wind speed indicator on the rear bulkhead, and he had glanced over his shoulder at it for a second, during the height of the blow. He had seen it reading 65 miles per hour. With his high speed, he had hitched up and made a straight line for Castries, which was why I hadn't seen him when the weather had cleared. We both agreed it was the damnedest thing we had ever seen. I never anchored in Anse des Pitons again. I have been told since that such storms can and do happen there at anytime.

Our schedule next called for a leisurely cruise at idle speed through the bay, then a turnaround to head north and back toward Castries. We repassed Soufriere, only from farther off shore, as we were not going into the bay. This course provided a new and equally lovely view of the little town. We then rounded up into another little bay called Anse Chastenet, where I grabbed a mooring line attached to a heavy cement block on the bottom, about 10 feet down.

I had found the block while scuba diving in the bay. Later, I had been told that it had been put there in connection with the construction of a nearby hotel and had long been forgotten about. I had put chain and a 3/4-inch nylon line on it and had added a float. Anse Chastenet was not as picturesque as Anse des Pitons, but it was infinitely more safe and, with the mooring block, I could eliminate tedious and risky anchoring. The swimming and snorkeling were good and the beach was even better. We were in very shallow, very clear water, right over coral formations. Those who were too timid to go in swimming or snorkeling could simply look over the side. There was always a magnificent display of multicolored tropical fish, and many types of coral, sponges and spiney black sea urchins could be seen. The guests loved the swimming and often came back with a souvenir sea shell. Sand dollars were everywhere, and even the most inexperienced would come back with at least one or two. A little touch that I insisted upon was to have my crewman standing by the swimming ladder with a tray full of rum punches as the guests came out of the water. How they loved it!

Oddly enough, people will stay interested in swimming for only about twenty minutes. Rarely did I have to call anyone back to the boat when it was time to move on. We would count noses again, pull in the swimming ladder and let go the mooring line. Backing away from the line, I would head north again, retracing our morning course down the coast. By then, everyone on board was exhausted. They had had a lovely, relaxing cruise down the coast, a tour through a new and unusual countryside, a West Indian dinner, a close-up view of one of nature's more remarkable landmarks, a swim in the most interesting and beautiful water many of them had ever seen, and had just been handed another rum punch. I knew that I had a happy bunch of people on board. They had about an hour's cruise to the next and last stop, Marigot Bay, and most spent it half asleep, soaking up the sun.

That was the good part of the day for me. All the often difficult parts of the day were over. We had survived another hassle with the jetty at Soufriere, the taxis had shown up, Mrs. Allain had managed to keep the lunch moving so that we weren't behind schedule, we had had no trouble picking up

91

the mooring (Ramshen once had fallen off the bow, boat hook and all), there had been no mechanical problems, and we were on our way home. It was quiet and peaceful, and I was left alone. I would often let my crewman steer the boat because I was tired of it by then. They all liked to do it, and it was good training for them as well. While I never taught any of them how to dock *Visitor*, they all were trained to operate the controls and to steer. If anything ever happened to me, they could get the boat back to Ganter's and call out for help from the marina.

As we turned into Marigot, someone usually awakened, saw the beauty of it, and began to rouse the others. Marigot was a curious bit of water. There was an outer bay which was lovely enough, but, at the inner part of it, there was a narrow opening into a small, but totally captivating lagoon, which was also part of Marigot. It had a mangrove swamp on one side and a small hotel fronting a beach on the other side. There quite often were blue heron stalking about the mangrove.

It was my habit simply to idle past this spot, as there was nothing to do there but look at the scenery. We then headed for Castries, about a 45-minute cruise farther up the coast. Coming into Ganter's, I would have the fun of executing another of my superb docking maneuvers, keeping a greedy ear cocked for the customary comments . . . "Christ, Martha, he handles this thing like it was a Volkswagen!" . . . "Cheez, did you see him bring this thing in?" . . . "Nice job, Captain." Well, it helped. I never once let on that I had approached the dock so many times that I could do it in my sleep.

I had bought *Visitor IV* because I had been fed up with my life-style and my work, because I had always wanted to live on board a boat, and because I had liked to fix things and make them perform properly. Chartering I did because I had to. But I can tell you that at the end of a day charter with *Visitor*, even chartering didn't seem so bad. By the time my crewman had her tied up and the shore power reconnected so that I could kill the engines and the generator, most of my charterers would have assembled in the salon to gather their belongings. I would come down the steps from the wheelhouse into the salon and be greeted like a long-lost member of the family at a family reunion. They *had* had the day of their lives and they would all try to outdo each other in expressing their thanks and appreciation. It happened hundreds of times during the years that I owned *Visitor,* and it never once lost its sparkle for me. It made me feel good as hell and there is no other way to describe it. Never, not once in more than ten years in the business world, did I ever receive the slightest fraction of such a reception for work I had done.

Guests would press their traveler's checks into my hand and ask if my charge was really enough. They would try to tip me; I always told them to give it to my crewman. They would invite me to have dinner with them at their hotel that night. They would call the next day with the names of people they had talked to about the trip who wanted to go. I would see them in town later on and they would greet me like an old college roommate.

Well, I guess we all need this kind of thing. It's part of our make-up. We need to be able to do what we enjoy doing and what we can do well, and we need to be recognized for it.

After they were all gone, when my crewman had picked up the empty glasses and the forgotten bottles of suntan lotion, towels, beach hats and so on, and he had put away the bow cushions and washed down the decks and gone home himself, I would sit down for the first time in ten long hours and have a drink—the first one and the best one of the day.

In day chartering, as in anything, there were good days and bad days. The good days seemed to melt together into a sort of nondescript mass, but the bad days left vivid memories. And there was always the worst, the very worst day ever. My worst was what I have come to call The Day of The *Jylland* (pronounced you-land).

The *Jylland* was a 130-foot Baltic three-masted topsail schooner with a black hull and white trim. She was powered by 5,000 square feet of sail, according to those willing to believe in that sort of thing, but, in fact, she had buried deep within her cavernous hull, a three-cylinder diesel engine. This monstrous piece of machinery had pistons whose diameter could more conveniently be measured in feet rather than inches, and its revolutions per minute were best measured by simply counting the exhaust explosions. When the engine was running, which was anytime the great thing was under way, it made a sound like a tuba in a German beer garden band—oompah, pah pah, oompah, pah pah. On a calm day, each explosion would send a perfect smoke ring rolling out the end of her exhaust stack.

I saw this monstrosity for the first time one day when it oompah, pah pahed its way down Vigie Creek, monopolizing every bit of water. It was headed for the fuel dock, and its skipper clearly had every intention of tying up. By the time he was off the end of the dock, he had drawn something of a crowd, for *Jylland* was certainly the longest apparition ever to arrive at Ganter's. He continued to oompah, pah pah right past the lot of us and down the side of the jetty. After what seemed like an eternity, at the last moment the pitch of the engine deepened, the oompah was eliminated and replaced by a continuous, loud, almost crackling pap, pap, pap, pap, pap. The exhaust gave up on the smoke rings and began to belch black smoke in earnest.

Suddenly, huge hawsers were thrown at those of us on the dock from what seemed like every possible point along her rail. We heard them hit the dock but didn't think to do anything about them, because, by then, we were all watching the *Jylland*'s 30-foot long bowsprit. Grace Ganter's pride and joy was the huge, plastic, illuminated sign that the Esso Company had put up on the shore at the head of the fuel dock when they were awarded the fuel business at Ganter's. That day was to be its last, because the *Jylland*'s bowsprit was aimed dead center at the O in Esso. One second later, with the accuracy of a Black Forest bowman, the *Jylland*'s bowsprit impaled the sign right through the letter "O". It was a sign of things to come.

We all fell to the lines, the *Jylland* backed away from its kill and, eventually, the great beast was secure against Ganter's trembling dock. Completely nonplussed by his deadly accuracy, the man at the wheel came to the rail, looked at the sign, looked at us and said, "Bloody hell! We hit it dead center, didn't we!" He looked like one of those Greek gods we lesser mortals have always heard about. Tall, built like a gorilla, deeply tanned and about 30 years old, Mike Atkinson had a mop of wild yellow hair and was wearing nothing but a pair of swim trunks. He beamed his cherubic smile down on us and asked, "Who's in charge?" We told him where the marina office was, and he bounded over the rail and was gone.

Outside, the *Jylland* was not a thing of great beauty and had never been intended to be so. She was more than sixty years old and had been built in Denmark as a coastal trader. We were to learn from her gregarious captain, Mike Atkinson, that she had been purchased several years ago by his employers, who were successful businessmen, all brothers, in England. They had spent untold thousands of pounds, according to Mike, rebuilding the *Jylland* to her present pristine condition. We were all pretty skeptical until we were finally invited aboard. True enough, belowdecks money clearly had been spent. There was a substantial bar, a built-in dining table and lounge area, and a number of quite nice little staterooms. The galley had been completely rebuilt, although it had the look of a restaurant kitchen. Stainless steel was everywhere.

All the new Formica, imitation leather, stainless steel and other modern materials used in the rebuilding clashed with the handsome old floor timbers and interior cargo planking which were allowed to remain. But, overall, it was impressive inside.

On deck, she really did look like an old sailing ship, in spite of the fact that it took gale force winds to get her up to steerage way under sail. The deck was rough and rugged and the planks were sealed the old-fashioned way with hot pitch. She had an immense windlass with wooden capstans that could take chain or line. To operate it, two men had to heave on either end of a great horizontal bar, which seesawed up and down to work a ratchet-like drive device. One up-and-down swing would bring aboard about half of a link of chain.

Her huge bowsprit carried three headsails, the main had a yard for a square sail and all three masts carried topsails. Very impressive, if you like that sort of thing.

Jylland's crew of ten were mostly British, except for a wild Australian couple and an American girl. They had had a long, tedious crossing from England, and had been in Barbados for the last six months, trying to day charter. There was a lot of speculation about just why they left Barbados, but their story was that there hadn't been enough business. Rumor had it

that there had been too much monkey business, including trying to encroach on some of the established, locally-owned day
charter territories.

Day chartering is a strange business. First of all, you cannot
undertake gainful employment in any foreign country that I
know of, without a work permit. The reason is obviously to
protect the jobs of the country's own nationals. And work per-
mits are generally not granted in areas of employment where
there are locally qualified people. One could not hope to go to
England, for example, and get a job as a teacher, secretary or
truck driver. They have hundreds of qualified British citizens
looking for those jobs. On the other hand, if you were a computer programmer and wanted to work at a computer installa-
tion in St. Lucia, where there probably isn't a qualified St.
Lucian programmer, the government would probably grant
you a work permit. But, if a qualified St. Lucian computer
programmer shows up, he can challenge your permit. It will
probably be revoked and the St. Lucian will get your job. And
why not?

What about day chartering? A couple of things. First, if you
are day chartering with a boat worth thousands of dollars and
carrying large numbers of people, you are probably doing a
job that no other St. Lucian can do. There was, at the time I
was in St. Lucia, no St. Lucian who chose to do day chartering
with a boat the size of *Visitor IV*. Secondly, living aboard an
international yacht, you are, in theory, not working on the Island anyway. It's all very vague, however. After all, the Island
belongs to the St. Lucians, as they are quick to tell you, if they
are in danger of losing an argument on any subject, and they
can do what they want to.

The key to it all is simple: don't get greedy and don't tread
on other people's toes, and, for the most part, they will leave
you alone. I suspect the *Jylland* gang might have missed this
point and found themselves in a situation where it seemed
best to get out while the getting was good.

All this also meant that, without any legal status on the
Island, I couldn't do a damn thing when the *Jylland* tied up at
Ganter's and decided to go into the day charter business. I

now had competition and plenty of it.

I still had a good edge, however, although I didn't realize it for some time. The *Jylland* had two drawbacks. One, it was not the most comfortable place to spend the day for the less-than-hairy-chested set. If the sails were up, then the protective canvas awning had to be down and that made it hot. Secondly, the great beast was so slow that it couldn't duplicate my route to Soufriere and the Pitons and get back the same day. One of my main selling points was that *Visitor IV* was the most comfortable way to get to see the sights at Soufriere: the mineral baths, sulfur springs and pitons. The road to Soufriere from Castries was hellish. The taxi drivers who took tourists there were their own worst enemies; they drove like Kamikaze pilots and scared the tourists away in droves. Usually, incidentally, in my direction.

And so it was that the *Jylland* went into business, doing a monotonous trip halfway down the coast into a little bay where they stopped for swimming and returned. But she was a sailboat, and sailors were accustomed to being bored and going nowhere in the hot sun. It was in their make-up. Some even liked it.

In the early days when *Jylland* first went into business, I was bitter and resentful about it. I had worked long and hard to build a following on St. Lucia, and there hadn't been much. Now, it looked as though I would lose the whole thing. Even that wasn't so bad. After all, that was one of the risks you took when you went into business. What really hurt was that *Jylland* belonged to three brothers, all English and all very successful and wealthy according to Mike. *Jylland* was a toy that they had bought to play with. Somehow, they had thought that there was a contract for *Jylland* to be used soon as a prop in a movie being shot on location somewhere in the West Indies. So, they had sent *Jylland* across the Atlantic. In the meantime, "Why not pick up a few extra dollars day chartering?"

They needed the money like a hole in the head and I needed it badly.

Mike and his young crew were a likeable bunch, full of fun

and having the time of their lives. In a reserved sort of way, we all got to know each other. Of course, none of them were responsible personally for the situation which I felt, at the time, was going to put me out of business.

Mike was the happy-go-lucky sort who would rush pell-mell into the middle of anything, manage to make a mess of things and then, somehow, come out smelling like a rose. He skippered the *Jylland* as though she were a London taxi, whipping her into tight places, running her aground and sideswiping other yachts. He always thought boating was one great big lark.

Of course, I was taking my chartering seriously and trying, perhaps too hard, to do it right. I liked him as a person, but had no respect for him as a skipper, and I loathed his boat. It was fertile ground for conflict, and it got its chance one morning. I had a lead on a large group from one of the hotels that was looking for a day on the water. I had talked with their leader, who would have preferred to have kept his group together. I couldn't take them all because there were too many, so I proposed to break them up into two groups, going on successive days. He said he would let me know.

The next thing I knew, Mike had the charter. He could take them all at once, which they had wanted, but I was out a substantial amount of money. The morning they were to go, I sat in the stern drinking my coffee, licking my wounds, and watching the group charter file aboard *Jylland*. I saw the engine fire up and heard it go to work trying to back away from the fuel dock. Funny thing was, she wasn't backing. I went over to investigate. Among Mike's less than seamanlike habits was docking *Jylland* by coming up against the shore with the bow, then backing off a bit and tying up. It did no damage to a bow as rugged as the *Jylland*'s, but it was a sloppy way to do things. We didn't have much tide in St. Lucia: about a foot, as a rule. But we did have springs. It turned out that, the last time Mike had come in, the tide had been at its very highest. It was now at its very lowest, and he had about a foot and a half of bottom paint showing at the bow where it rested on the shore. He also had about fifty passengers wanting to know what the hell was going on. I was quietly ecstatic.

For half an hour, Mike tried every trick in the book. He pumped the bilges. He had everyone assemble aft. He had them run from one side of the boat to the other and back. He tried to swing the stern with the engine and rudder, but the bowsprit swung also, and it became entangled with the Esso sign again. Finally, Mike did what I knew he would have to do. I was ready for him.

"Look, mate," he said, sweat dripping from his face, "how about giving me a tow with *Visitor*?"

"Yeh, Mike," I replied. "I'll give you a tow, but it'll cost your owners one hundred dollars."

Mike's reply was unprintable. He was furious. He called all his crew together, and the lot of them jumped over the rail and onto the dock. I thought for a moment they were after me, but they descended on the Esso sign. They all took a grip on it and pulled it to the ground. They then reboarded *Jylland,* and, by swinging the stern back and forth, as they were clear to do with the sign gone, he was able to work the bow out of the ground that held it.

Towing Mike out would have been a normal boating courtesy, but, under the circumstances, I just wasn't up to it. Occasionally, I have felt bad about the way I acted, but not often, and, when I have, it has been for exceedingly short periods of time. Mike never forgave me.

We did learn to get along, however. We were both interested in diving and occasionally went together. After a while, it got to the point where, if I weren't busy and wanted a day off, I would go out with the *Jylland* and they did the same with me on *Visitor.* One particularly bright, sunny day when I was going down the coast with a good-sized group, I spotted the *Jylland* ahead of me. Mike had every bit of sail up and was moving along nicely. He didn't always bother with the sails, but I must admit that she did look good with them up. I called everyone's attention to her.

"Now, there's something you don't see any more," I said in a burst of altruism. "A real sailing vessel under way with every sail set to a warm Caribbean breeze."

We closed up behind her and everyone on *Visitor* was enjoying the sight. I then clamped down on my throttles and swung to starboard to pass *Jylland*. There, on her port side, was that giant engine exhaust stack, blowing out its usual smoke rings. Everyone on *Visitor* turned and looked at me.

"Well," I said, "I tried."

Eventually, we got to the point where, if I were to hear of business that I couldn't possibly handle, I would tell Mike about it, and when he had too small a group for *Jylland*, he would send them to me. Not that this happened very often, mind you.

One such occasion, I would prefer to forget. Beverly was away on her annual trip to see her parents in Canada, and I was keeping an eye on things in her office. It was off season and there wasn't much going on for anyone. An overseas call came in on Beverly's phone and, thinking it might be some business, I took it. It was from a promoter in Miami who had organized a tour on one of the Cunard cruise ships that stopped regularly in St. Lucia. He said that he would be aboard next week with 125 people and he wanted his group to have something to do during their one-day stop in St. Lucia. Did I have any ideas?

The cruise ships all operated that way. They cruised at night, arriving at a different port each morning and leaving in the afternoon. I had been trying for more than a year to get business from the cruise ship lines without success. The lines that did answer me would tell me to contact their local agent; the local agent would tell me to write the line directly. No one really gave a damn because there wasn't enough money involved in the commissions. Ten percent of my little two hundred dollar day cruise for the ship's passengers wasn't worth the time to collect it.

Well, I certainly had some ideas, so I told the man in Miami that I would call him back within an hour with some specifics. I went off to find Mike. I knew he could carry 100 passengers and I could take the remaining 25, which was a boatload for me. The problem was timing. The *Jylland* was too slow to keep up with *Visitor's* usual schedule of activities, but Mike and I put our heads together and worked out a plan.

We decided to whisk the group down the coast to Soufriere, have lunch and whisk them back. No swimming, no ground tour, no Pitons, no Marigot Bay.

Mike and I calculated that, if we were to load the *Jylland* first and get it under way while I loaded, and if he were to milk everything he could from the engine and hoist every rag he had, he would get to Soufriere at about the same time I would. He could tie up and unload first.

There was another restaurant in Soufriere which could handle the large group if it wanted to. I had used this place when I had first come to St. Lucia because it had looked more impressive than Mrs. Allain's guesthouse. However, it was so badly managed that often there wasn't any food. And when there was food, the service was so poor that lunch took too much time out of the day. So, I had turned to Mrs. Allain. Mike and I hoped that by telling the owner of the place that there would be 100 people, he would make an effort to come through. I was to take my 25 guests to Mrs. Allain.

Fortunately, the cruise ship involved was one of the smaller ones that tied up at the banana ship docks in the harbor. Large ships like the QE2, the *France* and others visited St. Lucia, but anchored out and sent passengers ashore in the tenders, a time-consuming process.

Because we could pick the group up at the dock right beside the ship, there would be no delay in getting started in the morning. Dropping them off before their sailing time that afternoon would be easy as well. Cruise ships sailed on the dot, and they had been known to leave passengers who were not there on time.

It seemed like a workable plan. We conjured up a price that was low enough to be acceptable to a group, but left a little something for us. Since it was off season, it was better than nothing. We divided the price by 125, which gave us a per person split. By the time we had deducted Beverly's commission, because the call had, after all, come into her office, there was just about enough money in it for me to make it worth doing. Without all the extra chasing around, just a quick run to Soufriere and back, it would be OK.

I called Miami and told the man that we had planned a special, lovely cruise down St. Lucia's magnificent, lush, verdant coast to the picturesque little fishing village of Soufriere for a true West Indian . . .

"Cut the crap, fella," he interrupted, "I know all that bull better than you ever will. What's the bottom line?"

I told him our price and he wanted to cut it. I told him that, with the price so very low, we would have to eliminate the free rum punch. The deal was made and it was the biggest single mistake I ever made in St. Lucia. I should have stayed in bed that day.

The commercial docks at Castries were not really open to the general boating public. It was first come, first served, for the most part. Priority always went to the magnificent white banana ships that made the rounds of all the islands, carrying the "green gold" to England on a regular basis. I rather suspected that this priority might have been due in large part to the fact that the Geest Company, which owned the ships, had paid for the building of the docks, but I never could confirm this.

As luck would have it, and it was the first warning of a disastrous day to come, a Geest ship was loading bananas on the morning when our Cunard cruise ship, the *Adventurer,* was to arrive. This was no problem to the port officials. The cruise ship would simply have to anchor out, and that was exactly what she did. Mike and I figured the only thing to do was to go over to the dock and wait for the people to come ashore in the tenders. We put our radios on to work out docking between us.

My crewman and I had been ready for some time, so I fired up the engines and he attended to the lines. We backed out as usual and headed into Castries Harbor as the *Jylland* backed away from Ganter's fuel dock, which by now had become her permanent berth. As I approached the Castries dock, I could see that there was only one small open spot right under the bow of the huge banana ship. I relayed this to Mike by radio. Mike wanted to know if I thought I could fit in the space available and I said that I thought I could. We agreed that I would go in and tie up, then he would come alongside and tie to me. That way, 100 guests could cross over *Visitor* and board *Jylland.* Then *Jylland* could get a head start, while I took on the remainder of the group.

It made sense, but I didn't like the idea of acting as a fender for a 130-foot Baltic schooner, especially with something of a cowboy at her helm.

"Ah, Schooner *Jylland,* this is *Visitor IV,*" I radioed. "Look, Mike, take it easy coming alongside. I'm not the fuel dock and I bruise easily. If necessary, just get in close and we'll warp you in, over . . .''

"*Visitor,* this is *Jylland,*" Mike radioed back. "Don't worry about a thing, mate. We've got it all under control."

Mike made two mistakes. His first was to approach me into the wind at such an angle that the wind carried his bow and made an already hard-to-steer boat even more unmaneuverable. Instead of veering off to come up parallel to me, he came closer and closer, at virtually a right angle to my hull. His menacing bowsprit was pointed dead at my wheelhouse. He had had his massive rudder over for some time, but he hadn't been able to swing the stern in and the bow away from me. Knowing he needed steerage, Mike opened the throttle on *Jylland's* ancient, huge engine.

Just as the engine began to belch black smoke and change its tempo to the familiar pap, pap, pap, pap, a cry went up from several of the *Jylland* crew.

"The shrouds! Jesus, Mike, the shrouds!"

I couldn't imagine what they were talking about. I didn't know what a shroud was, at least not as far as boats were concerned. All I could think about or see was that godawful battering ram of a bowsprit heading for my wheelhouse, faster than ever, and showing no sign of veering off. I knew there was going to be a collision and that I had to get out of there fast. I dropped out of the wheelhouse and ran up on the bow where I hoped to be clear of the impact. The *Jylland* crew were making a dash for the bow of their boat, thinking perhaps that they could do something to lessen the blow.

105

Jylland had no gearbox; she reversed by way of a variable pitch propeller. Mike must have reversed her, for, as the bowsprit reached *Visitor*, *Jylland* slowed a little. I stood by helplessly as the bowsprit glanced off the outside corner of the wheelhouse. Behind it came the bobstay chain and dolphin striker. These began to demolish my beautiful mahogany cap rail, ripping out stanchions as they came. The tip of the bowsprit connected with the new cabinet I had had built to house the propane tanks. It was crushed like an egg speared by a pitchfork. The *Jylland*'s propeller was thrashing in full reverse pitch by now and her crew, at no small risk to their lives, were jumping from her bow down onto my deck. I rushed to join them and we all made a valiant attempt to push the bow away. Somehow, we were successful. The *Jylland*'s bow never actually hit my hull.

Several days later, we all had a lot of fun laughing about the only words that had been spoken during the crisis. As we had stood together on *Visitor*'s deck and had set our collective shoulders to *Jylland*'s massive bow in an attempt to deflect the blow, I had said, "I knew this wasn't such a good idea." It was the understatement of the year. Then Mike had come forward from the helm station after *Jylland* had been stopped. After surveying the damage without a word, he had said, in all seriousness, "I'll send the ship's carpenter over in the morning and set it all to right." It was the only time I ever saw Mike look concerned, but he overplayed his part to the point of being ludicrous.

When we did get *Jylland* tied alongside, we found the main cause of the collision. Mike had been right to gun his engine, but all he had succeeded in doing was to swing the stern enough so that the mizzen shrouds (the massive cables which supported the mast farthest aft) had struck the dock lines coming down from the huge bow of the banana ship. Mike, and indeed everyone else, had not seen the ship until it had been too late. The dock lines, coming from high above even the masts of the *Jylland*, had prevented Mike from swinging her stern in. The little bit that she did swing saved my wheelhouse from total destruction. As it was, there had been a ½-inch chunk taken out of the corner by the very tip of the bowsprit and the rails and the cabinet were repairable. Mike did have his crew do the work later that week.

When the dust, or perhaps the splinters, had settled, we began to wonder where the guests were. That they had not been standing by, watching the whole thing, came as an immense relief to all concerned. But where were they?

At last, an overweight man with a bloated red face came panting up to us and said, "Are you the guys with the boats?" Following along in his footsteps were the 125 souls who were to have the good fortune of sailing with us that fateful day. They were the lame and the weak; the strong, the vigorous; the Texan and the Ohioan; the butcher, the baker, the candlestick maker. They were overfed and overdressed, and they expected everything under the sun. They were behind schedule by exactly one hour.

They boarded without incident, which surprised me. I had been a little afraid that there might be a squabble about who would sail and who would come with me, but for some reason, those who wanted to sail hopped aboard the *Jylland* and those who sought class and comfort chose *Visitor IV*. The numbers were close enough to our plan to suffice.

It turned out that their leader had promised free rum punch, even though I had told him specifically that, due to his cut-rate price, there would be no drinks. So, everyone was unhappy within the first five minutes of the trip. The sea could have been nice and smooth, as it usually was on the lee side of St. Lucia, but there was a little one to two foot chop, and that helped not at all. I stayed behind *Jylland*, even though I could have passed her, because it was imperative that she dock first. She went in to Soufriere Bay: pap, pap, pap, pap.

On top of all the trouble we had had so far, the Soufriere jetty was packed. Sometimes a small freighter would be there unloading cement and lumber, or an inter-island schooner taking on copra, or the Island's commuter boat, which ran from Castries to Soufriere almost every day. Today, the whole jetty was taken up by all three. Mike had no choice but to go

107

alongside the freighter. The guests would just have to climb aboard, walk over the cement and around her cargo hatch, and down the boarding ladder on the other side to the jetty.

I lay off the jetty while Mike tied up and then came right alongside him. By the time my gang was ashore, his was out of sight, headed for the big restaurant. I led my group to Mrs. Allain, and, bless her heart, she had brought in extra help and was ready to go when we got there. When everyone had sat down and was eating, I began to wonder what luck Mike was having.

I left Mrs. Allain's and sauntered down the street to the other restaurant. When I arrived, I was shocked to find 100 people milling around like so many lost sheep. The tables were set but there was no food on them. A few people had drinks and that was the only saving grace in the whole horrible sight. The restaurant was owned by an American who preferred to leave it in the hands of a manager best described as a total incompetent. I had hoped against hope that with 100 guests expected, the owner might be there. I asked and he wasn't. I virtually shrieked for the manager. Taking him by his collar, I told him to get some food on the tables or I would serve him to the assembled multitude with an apple in his mouth and cloves all over his nether regions.

"But Mr. Bob, they haven't had their drinks yet," he replied.

I could have killed him and the owner as well. I had explained how critical time was for this group, and he was deliberately delaying the food to build up the bar tab. I reiterated my position. The look in my eyes must have told him that he had gotten as much bar business out of this group as he was going to. The food was on the table in minutes. By the time we got the group back to the boats, they were even more unhappy at having been rushed. And we were nearly two hours behind schedule. I could just see the cruise ship captain up-anchoring and sailing off without us.

I backed away from *Jylland* and waited for her to back from the jetty. She didn't. It appeared she was being carried in toward shore by the little swell that was running that day. I called Mike on the radio.

"Schooner *Jylland*, this is *Visitor IV*. You all right?"

"Visitor IV, this is *Jylland*. My reverse won't work."

Evidently, Mike couldn't change the pitch on his variable pitch propeller. Perhaps the hammering he had given it while trying to avoid cutting me in two earlier in the day had jammed something. As I began to return to help him, he managed to back out by himself. I swung away from him and we started back to Castries. Over the radio I told Mike I would head back full-bore and try to keep the ship waiting for the slower *Jylland*.

When I was in sight of the cruise ship, and let me say that I was as surprised as I was happy to see it there, I had a brilliant idea: why not put the passengers right on board the ship? If tenders could come alongside its gangway, surely we could too, and it would save precious time. I wanted to communicate with the ship anyway, so I took a long shot and dialed the international distress and calling frequency, 2181 kHz, on the radio and pressed the mike button.

"Cunard *Adventurer*, Cunard *Adventurer*, this is the Motor Yacht *Visitor IV*, the Motor Yacht *Visitor IV*, 2182."

I hadn't really expected a call, but they did answer and we established a working frequency. I explained the whole situation to them and asked if they would wait and if we could disembark passengers directly on to the ship. I was asked to stand by for the Captain to come on the air. I thought, "My God, the Captain himself." We had kept the ship waiting almost two hours and he must have been fully aware of who the culprit was.

The radio came to life again and a deep and very polished British voice told me that yes, the ship would wait for the huffing *Jylland*, and that we could disembark directly on board *Adventurer*. Well, at least the skipper of Little Toot had talked with the captain of a seagoing ship.

Hoping to rescue something worthwhile from this day of days, I made one slow pass at the gangway of the *Adventurer*. I estimated its height above the water and gave my crew detailed instructions on how to rig fenders. I noticed how the ship's tenders had one man pick up a long line, hanging from the main deck high above, to hold their bow in, and how the coxswain snagged an upright post on the gangway for the stern. But I had only one crewman, so I chose to have him set out a brest line to snap around the post on the gangway. I would have to position the bow with the engines.

I approached the gangway again and made a flawless landing. My crew got a line on the post, and there we sat just as nice as you please. Too good to be true. I should have known there was something strange about the way we sat so nicely, but I was too busy watching passengers step off *Visitor* and onto the gangway. If one of them slipped, it would be time to fade off into the sunset. None did, however, and, in less than a minute, they were all aboard.

I took the first deep breath I had taken all day. It was too soon. I had noticed the St. Lucia police boat hovering about my stern and I knew what they were doing there. The police band quite often performed on board visiting cruise ships for those who preferred not to go ashore. The boat was waiting to pick up the band.

Because they were behind me, although not in my way, I decided just to go ahead rather than back away from the gangway as I normally would have done. In seconds, I was pinned against the hull of the *Adventurer*. As I continued going ahead, the forward part of my life rail bit into the flaring hull of the *Aventurer*. It was another school day. I just couldn't get away from the hull of that huge ship, and the only alternative was to scrape and rub down the length of it until I got clear.

What the schoolboy needed to learn was that the enormously high side of a cruise ship will cause it to lie with the wind, rather than with the current, unless the current is extraordinary. The current is still there, however. It was the current, running at right angles to *Adventurer*'s hull, that slammed me up against the ship. It was, in fact, the same current that had held me so nicely against the gangway, and I hadn't had the presence of mind to recognize it.

When I had cleared the *Adventurer*, I radioed Mike to let

him know what the score was. I told him what had happened to me, and what I had concluded the cause to be. Mike then called the *Adventurer* himself and advised them of the problem. Could the *Adventurer's* tenders take the passengers from the *Jylland* and ferry them to the *Adventurer?* They said they would. With masts and rigging to worry about, Mike couldn't risk any collision with the *Adventurer*. It took even more time to accomplish this complicated transfer, but it was done and, finally, two and a half hours late, the *Adventurer* up-anchored and sailed for Martinique. While her captain and crew could not possibly have been happy with us, I shall always remember that they never complained and were very decent about the whole thing.

I headed for Ganter's. I was so exhausted that my hands were trembling. My mouth was bone-dry and my stomach in a knot. I remember trying to think of what else could have possibly gone wrong. Murphy's Law had put in overtime that day, and the paycheck would come due during the next week when we would work at putting the battered *Visitor* back together again.

Mike and I met on the fuel dock and just looked at each other and shook our heads. For once, the big, brawling Englishman could think of nothing to say. Neither could I. We were to joke about the whole horrible episode in the months to come, but not until a lot of the steam had gone out of us. We had made so little money on the whole deal that Beverly, after hearing the tale, offered not to charge us her commission. We accepted her offer.

My ten cents worth of advice to anyone even armchair dreaming about going into the day charter business is to tell the groups to get lost. You don't need them and they don't need you.

The groups I dealt with were invariably represented by a leader whose only motivation was the amount of commission he could get from the vendor (in this case, the charter yacht operator) under the table. He would sell his people down the drain to make a buck and would let them rot in their hotel rooms if there wasn't enough money in a day's activity to make it worthwhile for him, or, more often, her.

After forcing you to put on a bare bones performance by beating you down to your bilges on price, the group leader would return to the group and promise them the world with you as the supplier. He would tell them they would have a "full day" cruise, when he had knocked you down to a 10:30 to 3:00 shorty. He would include lunch, when no such agreement had been made. He would include the taxi fare from the hotel to the boat and return. He would talk about free rum punch, when you had told him it could not be offered at his price. He would say there was swimming from a beach to an elderly person who was too old to climb off the side of a yacht on a swimming ladder, when he knew full well that there were no docking facilities at the swimming area.

Having built up their expectations of the activities by say-ing, "Yes, of course!" to every question asked by his group, he would then announce a price far in excess of what the normal price for a full day packed with activities would have been. Because he had beaten the drum so well, and because he had credibility with the group as "The guy who knows his way around in these places", they would pay. The charter boat op-erator would be left holding the bag. Everything he didn't de-liver would be his fault. He would catch all the grief. And he would be paid peanuts for a hard day's work while the tour group leader would make a killing by doing nothing but what he or she did best: conning people.

In the beginning, I entertained the group tour leaders. I lis-tened in astonishment as they offered three or four dollars per person for a group of perhaps 10 or 15 or 20. My regular rate was twenty dollars per person which did not include ground transportation or lunch. I figured it wasn't worth starting the engines for less than $150. I did take *Visitor* out for a lot less than that in the early days, when I was trying to build a repu-tation with the hotel staffs. But once I got a reasonable follow-ing, I found that with a little scheduling, I could put a group of seven or eight together by asking individual couples what days they would be willing to go. Most were pretty flexible be-cause there was so little else to do for recreation in St. Lucia that their plans were not firm. Thus, when I got three or four couples waiting, I called them all up and scheduled a trip, usually for the next day.

Yet the group representatives thought that they were doing me a favor by offering me a large group, and that I, in turn, should cut my rates. Cut them, yes. Butcher them, no. A fa-vorite trick was to ask for a free day on *Visitor* "to evaluate the activity". That invariably meant that they would drink me dry of rum punch, I'd be stuck for their lunch at Allain's, and, nine times out of ten, I'd never see them again. I began to catch on to this after talking to some of the hotel managers. It was an old game that they had also used to get free hotel rooms.

One of the real joys of the little bit of success I achieved was that I no longer had to agonize over cut-rate groups. I would go as low as ten dollars for a guaranteed minimum of 15 guests, but I would give them the full day with the full program, so that no promises could be made that I wouldn't deliver on.

For about half a season, I had a good thing going with a nearby hotel. They were on contract to a Canadian tour group and would get a group of about thirty for a week, every week, back to back. The manager thought highly of both me and *Visitor IV*. He was also one of the very few in St. Lucia who took a direct interest in keeping his guests happy and busy.

Most of the managers either hid from guests behind paperwork, real and imaginary, or just didn't give a damn about them. "I've got a hotel to run here. I can't be taking up my valuable time trying to arrange entertainment programs. They'll just have to entertain themselves." I heard it time and again. I also heard them complain bitterly about guests that would book a week, then leave in three days for another island. The managers were too busy to recognize the obvious relationship between their attitudes and the guests' actions.

My manager friend and I set up a system whereby, the morning after a new group had arrived and settled in, he would call them all together in the outdoor bar area next to the pool. There he would give them a little poolside chat about St. Lucia and St. Lucians, taxis, church services, restaurants in town, and other helpful hints and a few dos and don'ts. He was so charming about it that they all took it in the helpful spirit in which it was intended.

He would then give me a brief introduction and recommendation, and I would talk about *Visitor IV* and our day on the water. I would tell them that, if at least ten people were to sign up, I would take them at fifteen dollars each. I almost always got 15 takers, and sometimes 20. It was a windfall. I never understood why it didn't last.

The manager was a Canadian and he was always there to greet the new group as a fellow countryman at the least, if not as a blood brother. They loved him for it. He always had a rum punch party set up for their arrival. While room assignments were being made and baggage being taken to the rooms, all the new arrivals had to do was to sit and listen to a steel band, drink free ice-cold rum punch and be greeted by a country-man. But, for some reason, after about two months, the travel tour group cancelled the arrangement, and that was the end of my windfall.

I hated to see them go for another reason. They were Canadi-ans, my favorite tourists. They always had such a good time without making asses out of themselves or getting into a drunken stupor. Not that they couldn't drink! It's just that they knew how to. A Canadian group would always ask thoughtful questions about St. Lucia, her people and govern-ment, rather than the usual rapid-fire, repetitive small talk. They always loved Mrs. Allain's from the first moment they saw it, without any of the initial skepticism that others often had. They would seek her out in the kitchen and thank her for such a lovely dinner. They all, always, went in swimming and often had to be called out when it was time to go. And they were my best salesmen when they got back to their hotel. I loved them.

I had another thing going for a short time with a bunch of wild people from the nearby island of Martinique. I was ap-proached on the boat one day by a deeply suntanned, athletic young man with a thick French accent. He was a tour group operator in Martinique and needed an off-island program for French groups on holiday in Martinique. A lot of his people had been expressing interest in a day's excursion to another island,and St. Lucia was closest.Could I do anything for him?

Of course I could, but running true to his breed's form, he wanted the world on a silver platter, at no cost, of course. He raised his palms, lifted his eyes to the sky and pled, "Ahh, but Monsieur, you are killing me!" He was too late for that foolishness. With tears in his eyes, he agreed to fifteen dollars per person with a minimum of 10, but promised me a full boat of 25. I told him that for every full boat he got, I'd slip him an extra fifty dollars. I later found out that he sold the trip for fifty dollars per person. The chartered plane to bring them to St. Lucia probably ran him about ten dollars per head. That monkey was making a clean twenty-five dollars per person on the side, as well as being paid a salary from the tour agency.

I never did get the promised full boat, but they were interesting trips all the same. The first trip with 18 or 20 people went like clockwork. As we were coming back up the coast, my French tour operator came up to the wheelhouse. He obviously had something on his mind.

"How do you think the day went?" I asked him with genuine concern. I needed this kind of business, so I wanted him and his group to be happy.

"Oh, very well, I think. Very well. But, ah, tell me, monsieur, about ze swimming. Is it necessaire zat we stop at zat particular place? Is zere any little, ah, how shall I say it? A place zat is more private?"

Anse Chastenet, where I stopped for swimming, was a bay used by the hotel that is located there. Their guests were always on the beach, but there had never been a problem between them and swimmers from *Visitor IV*. I looked at the Frenchman for a clue to the problem. It was in his face. How stupid of me.

So, we made our swimming stop at Anse Couchon, a deserted bay, when my French guests were aboard, and they did their swimming in their birthday suits. They had a lovely time and so did I. What more can I say?

It was unfortunate for both my morale and my bank account that this group didn't last for more than a month or so, either. I suspected that my greedy tour leader's price of fifty dollars each, or one hundred dollars per couple, had been a bit steep even for the fun-loving French.

There was another source of groups that was as disappointing as anything that involved *Visitor IV* during the nearly three years that I owned her. I have always prided myself on my uncanny ability to recognize a spade as a device for moving small amounts of dirt from point A to point B and nothing more, and the concomitant ability to recognize the phonies of this race of people to which we all belong. Because of all this, I have not been one of the world's great diplomats. And so my friends, while of exceedingly high quality, have always been few. But I had hoped to have friends and acquaintances in St. Lucia and, because I recognized the strong national and racial feelings of the St. Lucians toward outsiders, I had expected that my friends would be from what was known as the expatriate community.

Expatriates are a strange breed of cat. I know, because I was one when I was a news correspondent in Southeast Asia for two years, and when I was a charter yacht skipper in the West Indies for three years. There is a simplistic definition of expatriates as those who couldn't make the grade in their own country. This is perhaps true for about 25 per cent of them, and it is that 25 percent which gives the rest of us our unsavory reputation. But for every one who is an expatriate because he couldn't make it in his own country, there is one who elects not to make it in his own country for good reasons. These become expatriates out of choice.

The remaining 50 percent are simply away from home for a multitude of reasons: to escape a wife, or even several of them; to avoid the law; to do good works; to get a job; to make a lot of money; to avoid taxes; the list is long.

The curious thing about expatriates is their social groups. I am not a social scientist; in fact, I'm not even sure I like social scientists. But, on the face of things, one would think that expatriates would ban together. They are all in an alien land, usually distrusted and disliked by the natives, and always misunderstood. They have little knowledge about even the simplest of things, such as the best place to shop for a particular item, not to mention the customs and formalities of the country and its people. They often look and sound different, so that they are objects of attention, if not outright ridicule. They are frequently exploited. Because of all this, one would think that they would need each other. Let me tell you: as a group, they do not.

Rather, they divide themselves into very small, very tightly-knit subgroups, based on their broadest reason for being an expatriate. While it might be logical for all the wife-avoiders, or all the lawbreakers, or all the lonely divorcees to form a group, this is not the case. Instead a group is made up of all the Cable and Wireless (the British version of America's Ma Bell) employees, or all the hotel staffs, or all the diplomatic corps, or, yes, all the yachtsmen. The group boundaries are rarely, if ever, crossed. Thus Cable and Wireless may give a party, but you can be sure that there will be no one there from the yachty set at Ganter's.

It goes further than that, sadly. There is great antagonism between these groups, and many will not speak to each other on principle. Thus, you might hear reference among those in the British Government Representative's office (the best we could do for a diplomatic corps) to "the Cable and Wireless wives . . . oh, my, yes . . ." There was something decidedly un-healthy about the whole thing. It was kind of "dog eat dog", when we should have been working together as a pack.

All this doesn't have much to do with day chartering, but I had had the hope that I could find a little business and per-haps some social life among my fellow expatriates. I put the word out that *Visitor IV* was available for expatriate groups at half price. A pretty good offer, after all. While it was de rigueur for an expatriate to cry poor, they and I knew that we were being paid at least as much salary as we would have gotten in our native country, quite often with a not insignificant bonus; that our furniture and our cars were in company-paid storage or had been shipped company-paid to us; that we were often given housing at low or no cost; that the local cost of living was a fraction of what it was in our native country, and so on. In those rare places where any of these vast economic benefits do not occur, substantial bonuses were invariably paid. When I was in Saigon, where the cost of living was high, I knew com-

119

puter programmers who were getting a 100 percent "override", as it was called. Normal salary times two is another way to describe it.

If there were precious little to do on St. Lucia for the tourists, there were even less things for the expatriates. We had seen every hotel inside and out. I knew a couple that occasionally left their perfectly lovely home and booked into one of the hotels for a weekend, just for something to do. And we knew the eateries backward and forward. A day on *Visitor* at ten dollars a throw seemed like a natural. I kept the price low partly as a courtesy and partly to get regular, repeat business. I got virtually nothing.

In almost three years, I had probably ten expatriate group charters. Most were organized by Beverly who was something of a social butterfly and had managed to penetrate many of the cliques. After every one, I would storm down to her office and holler, "Never again, Beverly, never again." There was something about this clannish way of living which seemed to bring out the worst in every one involved. Going out on *Visitor IV* apparently was crossing the clan lines. If it were the hotel clan that Beverly had talked into chartering *Visitor*, for example, they would be crossing the line into the forbidden yachting-Ganter's clan. They would break the boundary out of desperation for amusement, but they then would proceed to take it out on me and the boat.

As a group, their attitude toward me was grumpy at best and openly belligerent at worst. They would treat my boat worse than the most outrageous tourist would. They would sit on the upholstered furniture in wet bathing suits. They would drop burning cigarettes on the deck. They always brought picnic lunches because they couldn't "afford to eat at Allain's", and they always left hard-boiled eggs, mayonnaise, cheese, ketchup and the like ground into the decks and carpeting. They, without exception or exaggeration, drank four times the free rum punch that a tourist group of comparable size would. They often got drunk and, as a result, did damage to the boat and my nerves. I was sure one of them would go off the bow while we were under way. There was always some clod in the group, who, after swimming, would take a shower in my head, and, after using my towels, deodorant, electric razor and who knows what else, would leave the mess "for the maid to clean up". I once found that a couple had used my bunk for its second best purpose at some time during the day. They always gave me a hassle when I tried to collect money from them. I never once had a tourist leave without paying. Expatriates did it any time they could get away with it.

I finally did draw the line one day. One of the little touches on *Visitor* that I liked was a sterling silver cream and sugar and tray set that I had out on the drop-leaf mahogany table in the salon. It had been given to my parents at their wedding and my mother had passed it on to me. The day that an expatriate charterer put his cigarette out in the sugar bowl was *the* last day I did an expatriate charter.

I really believe their behavior has something to do with group dynamics, and I base that on another interesting observation. Once in a while, often enough to make a valid comparison, an individual expatriate or two, such as a couple, would want to go on *Visitor* with a scheduled group of tourists. Perfectly pleasant, polite, and considerate: you couldn't tell them from the tourists.

One of the hazards of living on a boat was the loss of the privacy available in a land-bound house. No one in their wildest dreams would walk across a lawn and look into the living room windows. If someone did, the owner of the house would feel quite justified in going outdoors, taking them by the neck and rapping them in the nose, or, perhaps, having them arrested as a Peeping Tom.

But, although boating people know better, for some reason, non-boaters invaded privacy aboard as a matter of course. They thought a boat was just another tourist attraction, open to the public at no charge. Thus, it was not uncommon for me, as I was placing a forkful of dinner into my mouth while sitting at my dining table in the salon, suddenly to be aware that there was a face or even a whole family of faces, about two feet from my own, looking in the open salon window at me. It was

121

irritating as hell, but it happened so often that it had to be written off as an occupational hazard. I'd get mad, of course, and tell them to buzz off, or worse, depending on how the day had gone. But the evening was ruined from then on.

When I had the chance, I used to enjoy turning on the air conditioning on a Sunday afternoon and taking a nap for an hour or so. It felt good to get inside and miss the hottest part of the day, and, after a long week, it also felt good to rest. I would close the door leading from the salon to my stateroom, to conserve on the air conditioning, and leave the rest of the boat open. In fact, one of the little joys of living in St. Lucia was that I never had to lock the boat up. I could go out in the evening to the hotels, just closing the doors against possible rain, and the boat would never be disturbed. Except one time.

I was enjoying my Sunday afternoon nap with the air conditioning droning on when I was awakened by strange sounds from the salon. As a caution, I went to the door and put my ear to it. I could hear a number of people talking and laughing. They were clearly on board and in the salon.

In my fury, I threw open the door, forgetting completely that part of my Sunday ritual was to take my siesta in the nude. Air conditioning or no, it's hot in the West Indies during midafternoon.

"What in the damn hell do you think you are doing here?" I demanded in a blind rage.

When my anger parted enough for me to see what was before me, I was almost as astonished as my beholders were. There were about eight of them in all. They were all in their fifties, or older, and, obviously, by their look and dress, British tourists. There were two couples sitting on the sofa having their photograph taken by another gentleman. Another man was outside on the deck with his head stuck in the window, also taking pictures of those inside. One other had his head in my liquor cabinet and was eying my Mt. Gay Rum bottle. The last culprit was trying to figure out how to operate my high fi.

They all turned toward me and the women let out a scream that could be heard in Martinique. The men dropped what they were doing and, without so much as a word, took their shocked female companions by their trembling hands and fled as fast as their spindly legs would carry them. People are incredible.

The result of all this was that I had had to learn to protect my privacy, which I valued greatly, with more vehemence than might have been otherwise called for. If individuals who appeared to be tourists were to come down the dock toward *Visitor* when I had no charter scheduled, the hair on the back of my neck would stand up. Quite often, it would turn out to be a freeloader with his wife, who, under the pretext of considering going out on *Visitor*, would ask for a guided tour of every nook and cranny of the old girl and then disappear into the night, never to be seen again. He would want to see the engine room and have every pump and valve explained in tedious detail, while his wife would check out my closets and drawers. I closed the door of the refrigerator on the arm of one nosy bitch, who had gone too far.

With that kind of groundwork laid by the callous, the inconsiderate and the rude of the world, I was less than receptive one day when, as I was touching up a spot of questionable paint, a rather distinguished-looking couple began to saunter down my dock. By the time they had reached me, I had relaxed a bit. They were impeccably dressed, had a healthy, glowing, deep tan, and a look on their faces that radiated quiet confidence and gentility. There was an air about them that left me with the feeling that I was among my betters, on all counts.

The man introduced himself with a slight bow and asked if I were the captain. He spoke excellent English with a French accent. Well, "the captain" was standing there in his usual working attire: cutoff Levis and nothing more, save a little white paint on my thumb and index finger. I admitted, somewhat like the little boy admitting to taking a cookie from the jar without permission, that I was the captain.

"And this beautiful yacht, it is for charter, is it not?" he asked.

I had the feeling that this cat had bought and sold far more beautiful yachts than my poor old *Visitor*, but he had an honest manner. I said that *Visitor* was for charter, but that, unfortunately, at the moment I didn't have a group scheduled. It was the truth.

"Ah, but that is no problem. You see, we would prefer to not have others aboard. We would like to have the yacht to ourselves, if that is possible."

I began to think I was face to face with the charterer of my dreams.

"Well," I said, "it is possible, but it would be rather expensive. You see, normally we . . ."

"What would your charge be for the day?" he interrupted.

"Well, I really do not like to go out for less than a hundred and fifty dollars," I replied.

"Good," he said. "And we shall see you in the morning, then, at nine o'clock?"

I couldn't believe my ears. I began to stammer, "Of course. All the free rum punch you'd like. I'll include lunch at Allain's guesthouse." I was really feeling guilty about asking one person to spend so much.

"Ah," he said, "My wife and I do not drink, and we will bring some fruit with us for lunch. It is our preference. But, if you wish, perhaps you could make some kind of fruit drink for us. That would be very nice."

With that, he and his wife walked down the dock. Of course, any charterer who would pay a hundred and fifty dollars was a good charterer, but how I looked forward to having just two passengers to worry about. It would make my day so easy that perhaps, for once, I could relax and enjoy the trip myself.

That night Ross came by for a drink and I told him about my good luck. I mentioned the fruit drink they had asked for and he told me there was a blender on board his boat. Perfect. We had a great time rounding up mangoes, papaw, bananas, limes, oranges, grapefruit and more. We put the lot in the blender and let it whirl. The result was a little thick, but I thought that I could cut it with soda water as it was served during the day.

My charterers showed up exactly at nine and we were under

way in minutes. They were much more casually dressed, but with no sacrifice of taste or elegance. They went promptly up to the bow seat where, from the wheelhouse, I could just see their heads. I knew that, if they weren't going to eat in Soufriere, I had better keep my speed down in order to fill out the day. We had been going down the coast for about an hour or so, when I thought I would go up on the bow to chat with them and see how they were enjoying themselves. I turned the wheel over to my crewman and started forward. As I rounded the corner of the salon top, where the bow seat was, I realized why they had preferred to have the boat to themselves. They were soaking up the sun's rays and had made sure that no spot would go unblessed by that Caribbean warmth. Fortunately, their eyes were closed and they had not seen me. I beat a hasty retreat and spent one of the most pleasant days I was to have just cruising up and down the coast, while my guests did their thing in the seclusion of the bow deck.

Occasionally, the man would put on a robe and come back to the wheelhouse to ask for another two glasses of my fruit drink, which he was kind enough to say was the best he had ever had. Other than that, we never exchanged a word all day. We returned to Ganter's at the usual five o'clock and I was slightly relieved to see that they were dressed as we approached the dock. He paid me in cash, said they had had a perfect day, just what they had wanted, thanked me and walked down the dock. I never even knew their name. I have always wondered who they were and always will.

My biggest charter was the exact opposite in every respect from my smallest, although the initial contact was much the same. Once again, I was working on some project or other on *Visitor*, when a stranger came down the dock. The style and approach were different, however.

"Eh, captain, I vant to charter your boat!" was hurled at me in a thick French Canadian accent.

"Fine," I replied. I handed him a brochure and began to explain the need to get a group together.

"I have ze group. I have my friends, captain. How many can

125

you take?"

I told him that I preferred to take no more than twenty-five.

"But I may have thirty. Can you handle zat many?"

I couldn't pass that by, and, besides, twenty-five had always been a conservative number. I had had twenty-five only once before, and it had worked out well. I could handle five more. I would have to borrow some life jackets, but I knew where I could get them. I told him I could do it.

"Marvelous," he went on. "Now, we are at ze hotel in Vieux Fort. You can pick us up zere in ze morning, yes?"

Vieux Fort was at the southern end of the island, a good three-hour haul. I protested, saying it would be better if his group came to Castries by bus, but he would have none of that.

"All right," I said, "but I shall have to ask for a surcharge. That represents six hours of extra running time, down and bàck."

He agreed to a fifty dollar surcharge and never had the common sense to ask for a group rate. The job stood at $650 for the day. I was ecstatic. Little did I realize that I was to earn every cent.

"Now zen," he said. "My friends will need some drinks. Can you take care of zat?"

I explained that rum punch was included at no cost.

"No, no, no," he said, unimpressed. "My friends will require . . . can you write zis down? . . . two gin, two of scotch, two vodka, two rum, two brandy, let me see, some wine, some red, some white, some beer, perhaps four or five cases of different brands . . . no, it is better we get three of everything, I think. And ice, we will require plenty ice, yes? Now zen, about lunch, captain, what do you recommend?"

My mind was swimming, but I knew I had a live one on the line and I wasn't going to let him off the hook. Picking him up at Vieux Fort in the south, the cruise would have to go north and that meant right back to Castries. Directly in back of my dock, across the water, was the Coal Pot restaurant. It was owned and run by Bob and Sonya Elliot and they were a story unto themselves.

126

Bob, many years ago, had been the youngest person at the time, to cross the Atlantic singlehandedly in a sailboat. He had left from England and ended up in the West Indies, the route of many Atlantic crossings. He was the son of a wealthy New England family and, as such young men often do, he had told the family fortune to go find someone else to bother. He had liked it in St. Lucia and had stayed. It wasn't long before he met and married Sonya, the daughter of one of St. Lucia's leading families. He had needed something to do, so, wisely anticipating the tourist boom, he had built and opened the classiest and best restaurant on the Island. It was an open-air affair, right on the water. Had I not been careful when backing *Visitor* out of her dock, I would have put her stern in the Coal Pot's dining room. Bob had a long and questionable history on the island, and his spats with Sonya were the talk of the town. In one classic battle, Bob threatened to close the restaurant. He took out a full-page ad in the St. Lucia paper which said simply:

THE

COAL POT

IS

CLOSED

R. A. Elliot

A week later, in the next edition, there was a full-page ad which said simply:

THE

COAL POT

IS

OPEN

S. Elliot

Bob had never given me any trouble, and, in fact, when we had gotten to know each other he would always go out of his way to be hospitable and friendly. I didn't trust him any farther than I could throw him because of his reputation, but until he crossed me, as far as I was concerned, we had a clean slate.

I told my French Canadian that I did indeed have an idea about lunch and pointed out the Coal Pot to him. I suggested that we should go aboard *Visitor* and give Bob a call. I dialed and got Bob on the line. Trying as subtly as possible to let him know I had a hot one, I introduced my man and put him on the phone. The conversation as I heard it went something like this:

"Ah, yes, Mr. Elliot . . . I have my friends and zey will require lunch . . . something nice, I like to live well, you see. Cornish game hen? Yes, zats nice . . . yes . . . yes . . . Ah, Mr. Elliot, you understand me. That's good. And the wine, Mr. Elliot, I want it to be kept always at hand. Please don't force my friends to have to ask. You see, I like to live well. Yes, thank you, good-by."

He then turned, gave me three hundred dollars in cash and his card to seal the arrangement, and said he would see me in Vieux Fort in the morning. He left and I sat down. In seconds, Bob was shouting at me across the water asking me to come over. Naturally, he wanted to know what the score was on this nut. We kicked the tale around for an hour or so, then I left because I had a lot of work to do.

I sent my crew off to borrow extra life preservers from Ross, and I went in town to buy what turned out to be about two hundred dollars worth of booze. I also bought two large plastic trash cans. There would be no time to buy ice at the hour when we would have to leave to get to Vieux Fort by nine o'clock, so I had both cans filled with ice at the ice factory in town. I figured that by morning, the ice would have melted enough to make room for the beer.

I had long since replaced Andrew with a young St. Lucian whom I had known for some time as one of the boys at the jetty in Soufriere. He was older and wiser than any of them and I had thought it would be good politics to have a crewman from Soufriere. His name was Placid. So help me, that was his name. And he was one of the best crewmen I had. He learned well; he was polite and helpful towards the charterers to the point where he often got far more money in tips than his salary. I was glad to have him. Because of our early departure, I asked him to spend the night aboard.

By six the next morning, Placid and I were pushing south

for Vieux Fort, feeling more like a liquor store than a yacht. We tied up at the Vieux Fort jetty right on time, after a relaxing and delightful, early morning cruise. I was pleased that the water had been calm, because at times it could be choppy just south of the Pitons.

The gang arrived just a few minutes late, having been brought to the jetty by the hotel's bus. Loading, in spite of the huge crowd went well and, playing the good host, my charterer did his best to introduce me to everyone as they came aboard. He didn't seem to know the names of many of them; those he did know, he called by first names only. I thought it a bit strange at the time, but had too much on my hands to worry about who these people were. I was about to make the most money in one day that I had ever made, or ever was to make, and I wanted it to come off well.

One of the lucky things that never ceased to amaze me about large groups was the way they almost automatically spread out in the boat. I was invariably afraid they would all want to sit up on the bow or in the wheelhouse. But, everytime, those who wanted the comfort of the salon stayed there, happy just to look out the windows; those who wanted to be outside, but protected from the sun, gathered in the covered cockpit; and those who wanted to bake in the sun chose my open midships deck. So, thirty people walked aboard *Visitor* and found the spot they liked the best. We were off, with no one crowding any other person.

I had told Placid that these were drinkers and that his whole day would be spent getting drinks. I was right. We hadn't cleared the jetty before I heard the first beer can pop.

As we worked our way up the coast, everything was going just fine. They were all having the time of their lives, occasionally bursting into what I assumed to be Canadian national songs. The liquor flowed like water, but my charterer was paying for it, so that was his problem. At that point, at any rate.

Poor old *Visitor IV* must have been quite a sight when she steamed into Vigie Creek that morning. Thirty half drunk souls were manning the rails and singing the Canadian National Anthem, as we rounded up to Bob Elliot's Coal Pot dock. We tied up without a flaw and the mob descended on the Coal Pot, like prisoners breaking out of jail. Bob and Sonya had, of course, gone all out. There were flowers everywhere, including down the full length of the one, long banquet table, which had been set up. Thirty was about all Bob could handle, so the restaurant had been closed to the public. That was just as well.

I introduced Bob to the charterer and Bob was again reminded to keep the wine flowing. Good old Bob needed no reminding. I could see five cases of some of his best, stacked and waiting in the corner. His bartender and right-hand man, Iggy, was there in full regalia, and a few extra girls were visible out in Sonya's kitchen. Bob knew how to do things right.

I suspect that was one of the things I liked about him.

The feast was laid and the orgiasts assembled at the groaning board. For three hours, all I could hear was the sound of song, toasts to one and all and the pop of wine bottles. Everyone was having a superb time. The lunch was toasted as the best in the West Indies; the girls were prodded, giggling, from the kitchen and were toasted as the hosts with the most; and I, modest soul that I am, was toasted as the finest sea captain on the seven seas. Clearly, they were getting drunker.

I wanted to get into Vieux Fort before dark, so knowing it would be at least a three-hour trip back, I began to make suggestions that we break up the party and return to *Visitor*. My charterer went into a huddle with Bob, then peeled off a considerable amount of money from the ready supply he always seemed to have at hand, and the two of them shook hands. I never did get a straight answer out of Bob as to what he took in that day, but I did see the five empty wine cases piled in the corner. There had been no discussion of group prices with me, so I was sure Bob had gotten his going rate as well. That would have made the tab for lunch five hundred to six hundred dollars.

The lunch had somewhat subdued my songbirds and things were a little quieter as we steamed out of Castries Harbor and headed south. We had the time, so I did a quick nip into Marigot Bay for them, but not many saw it. By the time we got

130

to the Pitons, they had all come back to life and had begun to go after the liquor with a vengeance. I guess they realized the party was nearing its end and they wanted to milk it for all it was worth. The beer was gone, so they worked on the hard stuff in earnest.

I began to get worried. For one thing, we were getting into the kind of seas that were usual, south of the Pitons. It looked as though we were to pay for our smooth passages of the morning with a rough one that afternoon, the worst possible time. The waves built to two and three footers, nothing to worry about under normal circumstances, but enough to make *Visitor* roll and pitch a little. I had thirty passengers who were doing too much of that on their own without any help from the demons of the deeps.

Finally, *Visitor* stuck her bow into a wave and sent spray flying back the whole length of the boat. I throttled back, but she did it again. Of course everyone on the bow was soaked, but they thought it was a ball. I thought it was a potential disaster, so I turned the wheel over to Placid, after slowing the engines to an idle. I went up on the bow and, as politely as possible, asked everyone to come inside or aft, but, in any case, off the bow. There was a lot of kidding around and a lot of "Aw, come on, captain, we're having a ball!" I insisted, but they became more unhappy about the idea. As I kept insisting, a few began to get a little ugly about it.

I knew how to handle that. Our course had been right into the sea, which was why we were getting so wet. I got Placid's attention at the wheel and, with my arms, motioned for him to turn the wheel to port. I kept him turning until we lay right in the trough. Low in the water as *Visitor* was with all those people aboard she did one of her best 30 degree rolls. Thirty seconds later, I was the last one to leave the bow deck. Not another word had been spoken.

When I got back to the wheelhouse, my usually somber Placid had a smile on his face. I swung *Visitor* back on her proper course and we plodded along, while the group continued with the booze and song from within. It was slow going, because I didn't want anyone hurt below, as we pitched in

131

some very choppy seas. The sun had just gone over the horizon as I lined up on the Vieux Fort jetty. I could see trouble coming.

Tied up at the jetty were two freighters, each monopolizing a side of the jetty. I went around to the southern side and saw that I had a chance, but not much. There, tied up under the bow of one of the huge freighters, was Peter McDoom's 60-foot hotel launch. Next to it was the hotel's 45-foot sportfisherman. It was nothing for me to raft out third. After all, the 60-footer was steel and could take anything, and I had good fenders for the fiberglass sportfisherman. The problem was going to be getting thirty drunks over those boats and onto the jetty.

Placid rigged the fenders and set out the lines, then we went in alongside the sportfisherman. Fortunately, her crewman was aboard and he helped with the lines. I killed the engines and, with fear and trepidation, went down the steps into the salon. The smell of booze was overpowering, but the smell of wet, sodden bodies was also present. They were piled up on each other as though there had been a wave of plague. I stepped over and among them, looking for signs of life. There were few.

Placid was out on deck talking with the crew of the sportfisherman. I told the two of them what we were up against and offered the other fellow ten dollars if he would give Placid a hand in carrying the dead off *Visitor*, over the two other boats and up on to the jetty. From there on, they were on their own as far as I was concerned.

And so the process began. One at a time, the three of us would get a body on its feet. The two crewmen, one under each arm, would half carry, half drag the limp form outside and onto *Visitor*'s deck. I had an opening in my life rail at the salon door, and they went through that and over onto the fishing boat. From there, the path wound around the fishing boat's bow deck and up onto the hotel launch. Then, across the launch and up onto its bow. That, thank God, was about the height of the jetty, so it was an easy step onto it.

One by one, we did it. The crewmen thought the whole thing

was a panic and laughed and joked their way through it all. It was fortunate they were so good about it, because I could have gotten a little morbid about things. I liked to see people have a good time on *Visitor* and always felt bad when they got stoned. It made me feel that I hadn't done a good enough job of keeping them entertained, or making it possible for them to enjoy themselves without needing to get bombed. Of course, it wasn't rational, but the feeling was there anyway.

The last of the living dead was my charterer himself. He was still on his pins, actually, but as stoned as the rest. I put on my best cocktail party smile and sought him out.

"Well, I guess the day's over, isn't it?" which was my way of saying, "It's time to buzz off, old boy."

"S'hell it is, captain. It's just beginning and I'm having a lovely time! Have a drink!"

Oh, boy.

It was too late to try to get back to Ganter's that night, so I knew we would have to spend the night at Vieux Fort. I had never seen the hotel and had thought I would go there for a quiet dinner to celebrate my good fortune. And so, rather than argue with my sodden charterer, I went into my stateroom, took a shower and got changed for dinner.

When I returned, he was sitting on the sofa with a drink in his hand. He had evidently asked Placid to gather the unused liquor bottles for I could see them in a paper bag by the door. There were only about five or six bottles left. It didn't seem possible. I told him that I would like to go up to the hotel for dinner and asked if we could settle our account and close up the boat. I showed him a written account of what the liquor had cost, plus the charter fee, less the three hundred dollar deposit he had given me. It was perfectly agreeable to him. He reached into an old airline bag that he had been carrying around all day and pulled out, quite literally, a fist full of bills. There were Canadian and American dollars, West Indian dollars, French francs, and others that I couldn't identify. He thrust it all at me and said, "Snuf?"

I didn't actually know if it were "snuf", so I sorted out the American dollars until there was "snuf" and gave the rest

133

back to him. He put the remainder in the airline bag, zipped it shut, then did the one thing I thought he could never do: he stood up. He thanked me profoundly for the finest day of his life, bent over and picked up the bag of liquor bottles, and started for the door. Placid appeared out of nowhere and took his arm. At that point, the bag broke and the bottles crashed on the carpeting.

"Don't need any help, zank you very much," said he and, brushing Placid aside, he stepped through the door. I was so mad about the carpeting that I let him go. I bent over the broken glass and began to pick up the pieces. When I had gotten the biggest ones up, I took several old towels, placed them over the wet area and walked on them, hoping to soak up the liquor.

"Mr. Bob! Mr. Bob! Mr. Bob!"

I looked out and saw the crewman from the sportfisherman jumping up and down on the bow, calling my name. Knowing full well what to expect, I left *Visitor* and walked over to see what was going on.

"De man does be in de sea, Mr. Bob! Look me, just now!"

I looked in the water below the bow and couldn't see a thing. Suddenly, Placid's curly head broke the surface ten feet below us.

"Take de bag, Mr. Bob," he gasped.

I looked down into the darkness and saw he was holding up the airline bag in which my charterer carried his horde of money. I couldn't reach the bag anyway, but I said to Placid, "Where is the man?"

"He does be down dere, Mr. Bob."

"Down where?" I asked incredulously.

"In de sea, Mr. Bob."

"Placid, for Christ's sake, forget the damn bag. Get the man!" I cried.

By this time, the other crewman had gone for a boat hook and returned. He snagged the bag in a second and Placid disappeared beneath the dark water. Seconds later, he came back to the surface with my charterer. At this point, the other crewman jumped in the water to help. Together they worked him around to the stern of the fishing boat, but the freeboard was so high that I didn't have the strength to pull him aboard. I did get him high enough to be able to see that he was breathing, although, to this day, I have never understood why.

Tied up to the side of the hotel launch, there was an old rubber life raft that they used when painting the hull. I suggested they try to roll him into that, then pull the raft to shore. This they did with success and then half carried, half dragged, as his predecessors had been, my illustrious charterer was brought to the head of the jetty. We returned his airline bag to him, called a cab, stuffed him into it and sent him on his way.

I asked Placid what had happened.

"De man he jus walk right off de boat into de sea," was his reply. Exactly what I had suspected. I asked him why he went after the airline bag rather than the charterer. Placid may have been quiet, but he didn't miss much of what went on.

"De bag have de bread, Mr. Bob."

I gave them what was left of the booze, which I knew they could sell for a good price, and called a cab for myself.

When I arrived at the hotel, I just roamed around a bit, because I wanted to see the place. It looked like any one of a thousand large resort hotels, so I headed for the dining room. Just as I was entering the door to the dining room, I bumped into someone heading the same way at the same time. I turned to face my charterer. He was looking fit as a fiddle, cleaned up, shaved and in a white dinner jacket, tie, and black pants with a satin stripe down each side. I could hardly believe it was the same man.

"Captain! How good to see you again! You must join my friends and me for dinner!" He was insistent. It seemed easier to join him than to argue. I found myself sitting with the whole lot of them. While I was making small talk with a woman sitting next to me, it suddenly occurred to me to ask the question that had been in the back of my mind all day: who were all these people, "my friends"? Not wishing to appear too nosy, I said to her, "How long have you known this fellow who chartered my boat today?"

"Known him?" she replied. "We don't know him at all. We

all were on the same flight from Montreal to St. Lucia, and, by the time the plane landed, he had invited us all to be his guests for the day and now for this dinner. I don't even know his name.''

It has always seemed incredible to me the amount of tragedy, both in terms of loss of boats and of loss of life, that I experienced during my comparatively short time in the West Indies. I have already told of the loss of the lovely old Baltic Ketch during Race Week at PSV. And there was the near loss of the trawler yacht in Marigot Bay, which motivated me to install my bilge alarm.

These were church picnics, compared to the real tragedies where loss of life occurred. The worst of these happened when I had been in St. Lucia less than a year. One of the hotels maintained three or four outboard motorboats for the entertainment of their guests. These boats were operated almost daily under conditions which would bring fine and imprisonment in the United States and the wrath of God down on the conscience of the person responsible for them, no matter where they were. If he had a conscience.

I saw the remaining boats immediately after the tragedy and again some months later and they were in the same deplorable condition. They had no life preservers, no fire extinguishers, no lights, no signal flares, no radios, no anchors or anchor lines, no spare parts, no emergency motor, no supplies of fuel, rations or water. They had, in fact, nothing but a hull, seats, a motor and an operator.

I wondered whether the motors were properly maintained and the operators properly trained. A trained operator would know better than to take out a boat that lacked at least some safety equipment.

Late one afternoon, the word spread through Ganter's like wildfire. One of the boats had not returned with its operator and two guests aboard. Basically, when this sort of thing happened, it fell to the boating community to conduct a search and rescue operation. While St. Lucia did have a police boat, it was in operating condition less than half of the time and its communication equipment functioned even less often. It had been given to the state by the British government, but it had been so poorly designed that its heavy steel hull couldn't get up on the water, and its top speed was about nine knots. There was little money for maintenance and parts. Although she had a devoted crew, no one aboard had the foggiest idea of how to use the boat, with the exception of the boat's captain, who had received formal training and who fought a losing battle for funds and parts.

In a crisis, then, the unofficial and unorganized Vigie Creek Search and Rescue Flotilla would assemble to do what they could, which wasn't much. We did have some skill as well as useful boats and working equipment, but we had no radar for searching and no radio direction finder for homing in. We paid for our fuel and maintenance and time out of our own pockets.

We were a motley crew. Each of us tried to do our best, but we never had a leader, we had no chain of command or procedure, and no public or governmental support. People died because of it.

We had Bob Elliot and his 28-foot Bertram which gave us a cool head and a good navigator with a fast boat. We had *Visitor IV* which gave us me, for what I was worth, and an able, large boat with a 100-watt radio that could serve as a base of operations on the water. We had Mike Hackshaw and his

138

brothers, each with a boat of some kind and the guts to keep on looking after the rest of us were ready to give up. And we had Beverly, who would act as our shore link, using the radio she kept in her office for her charter work.

Some of the other power boat owners would help out if they knew there were an emergency, notably, Dan Flosac. Dan was missing part of one arm, but he could whip his 21-foot inboard-outboard around with the best of them. Dan and I worked together for a day, once, trying to locate an underwater scientific, electronic device, he with his boat and I with my scuba gear. I found it while literally on my last gasp of air, and I was damn glad to know it was Dan who was on the surface to help me when I came up.

On the afternoon when I got word from Beverly about the missing boat, I called Bob Elliot, told him the score and asked if he were willing to go out. Because there wasn't much daylight left, speed was critical and the slow *Visitor* wouldn't accomplish much. Also, Bob would need someone to look while he operated his high-speed boat. So out we went, the only two people in the world who were looking for three lost souls and we had almost no idea of where they were. It was interesting to note that the big, high-speed sportfisherman, which belonged to the hotel whose guests we were looking for, was tied up to its pier, its engines cold, as we sped out of the Harbor. We looked until it got dark and returned with nothing but an empty fuel tank.

The next day, by then too late for all practical purposes, everyone got into the act. The missing guests were Americans, so the U.S. Coast Guard sent two sea planes to the scene. A helicopter appeared from a British warship that must have been in the area. The pros searched for three days and found nothing. In fact, the boat and its three passengers were never found. With no safety equipment on board such as a flare or radio, there was nothing to look for except a tiny pinpoint of color on thousands of square miles of churning ocean. After the first sunset, it was a lost cause. Overnight, the boat, if still afloat, would drift so much that the area where it might be would become too large to search effectively, even with professional search aircraft. There was a hue and cry after it was all over. Everyone agreed that something should be done to prevent it happening in the future. But no one did anything.

While I was on the slipway having *Visitor*'s bottom cleaned and painted, there was another tragedy. A gang of young men had overloaded a small dinghy at Ganter's, then tried to row out to an anchored yacht. It was late at night, and, when the boat swamped and they all had to swim to shore, it was an hour before they realized one of their group was not accounted for. Those who knew how to scuba began a search in the morning, when there was light to see by, and, within an hour, they found his body and brought it to shore.

It was only a few months later when we suffered another loss. Rodney Blackman was a good friend of mine. He was assistant manager at one of the small, locally owned hotels, and an avid supporter of *Visitor IV*. He was not only a good friend but a godsend to my business. Rodney, in his quiet, British way, probably sent me more charterers than any other hotelier. He always insisted he was doing it only for the hotel guests. He felt they would have a good time on my boat, and the most important thing for Rodney was pleased guests. There were probably no more than six other people among the staffs of the Island's eight major hotels who shared his view, and Rodney's boss was not one of them. Rodney was constantly admonished by him for "not paying attention to the important things".

Late one afternoon, Rodney took out a sailfish sailboat, which was little more than a surfboard with a mast and sail, from the hotel's fleet. They are tricky for the novice to handle and will flip over easily. They are just as easy to right, but are inherently dangerous because if you don't hang onto the boat after it is righted, it may sail away from you. Rodney was not experienced with these little boats. He had been out in them only two or three times and what little he knew was self-taught.

There was one hour of daylight left by the time the hotel's beachboy reported to the manager that Rodney had not returned. Actually, all he reported was the loss of one of the sail-fish, for which he was accountable. He had not been trained to keep an eye on the users of the equipment, just on the equipment itself. When asked who had the missing sailfish, he told the manager it was Rodney. The manager was a friend of Bob Elliot, so he called him at once. Bob alerted me and the two of us took off in Bob's boat. Meanwhile, the manager alerted the Hackshaws and Dan Flosac, who got under way just as soon as they could.

I was sure we would find Rodney quickly. His mast and sail would be highly visible. He couldn't have gotten far in a sail-boat. We sped to the hotel's beach to get our bearings, then worked away from there. We ran out a mile or so, shut down the engines and called Rodney's name. We listened a while, then tried the same thing in another spot. It was dark by the time Dan and two of the Hackshaw boats were able to get out to where we were. We kept in touch by radio to try to prevent overlapping searches. But in the dark, it was impossible to tell what we were doing and where we had been, with any accuracy. We looked and we looked and we looked. We called. We listened. We compared theories over the radio. Might he have drifted north? Mike Hackshaw would check it out. How far south had Bob Elliot gone the last time? Should someone else go farther? Suppose he had slipped off the boat: did he have a life preserver? No.

By midnight, we all agreed we had been wasting our time from the moment darkness had fallen. Every little whitecap looked like a floating object, and any floating object would have looked just like another little whitecap. I have never known such burning frustration. Rodney was out there. He had to be. He could have been right beside the boat and, un-less the engines were shut off, we wouldn't have known it, even if he had beaten on the hull with a hammer. Twin gaso-line engines idle at 800 rpm, and their exhaust makes a hell-ish noise, even at idle. But he was there. Somewhere. In that blackness. He could even have been watching us circling around, looking for him. He might have seen us give up and watched our lights disappear into the Harbor.

What ever happened, we never saw Rodney again. We looked for two more days and had some help from other agencies. We sent messages to the other islands, as far as South America, asking them to report any sign of the unsinkable sailfish. There was never a trace.

Rodney's father came to St. Lucia to try to find out what had happened to his son. There was little to tell him except that a lot of us had done our best to find him. There seemed no point in saying that a minimum of safety training at the hotel might have prevented it. Just as nothing was changed at the other hotel after the three were lost, there seemed to me to be little chance that this hotel would take a lead in promoting water safety.

Bob Elliot took Mr. Blackburn out in his boat and Mr. Blackburn dropped a wreath in the water off the hotel's beach. He flew back to England the next day.

There were other rescue efforts which did not result in tragedy. One incident always seemed to follow on the heels of another. I remember being called to Soufriere one night to tow a disabled and sinking charter sailboat into Ganter's for repairs. A few days later, an old sailboat, which had been anchored in the little yacht anchorage between Vigie Creek and the Harbor, began to take on water. She was a sad example of what happened to an old lady with an absentee owner. I was no authority on sailboats, but I could recognize a graceful clipper bow and handsome joiner work when I saw it.

I don't remember who noticed her taking on water first, but on a Sunday afternoon, there were few people around to help. I expropriated a powerful outboard runabout that belonged to the *Jylland* and, with what few others I could find, dashed out to see what we could do. By the time the group of us got to her, she had settled to her portholes, which were leaking as badly as her hull must have been.

It seemed clear she would go to the bottom in a matter of minutes. She was in 25 feet of water; with the limited facilities in Castries, that would probably have meant the end of her. I didn't think there was any way she could have been raised.

On the other hand, she wasn't my boat and I had no authority to be messing with her. Still, there was only one course of action that I could see. We had no heavy pumping equipment at hand and time was short, so we secured the runabout to her side and let go her mooring line. Then, using everything the runabout had, I moved her inshore, until she touched bottom. She settled into the mud for a foot or so and then stopped in an almost perfectly upright position. A good wake might have toppled her over, but the Harbor was quiet.

After an hour, we were finally able to borrow a large, gasoline-driven water pump from a construction company at the north end of the Island. It was so huge that, when we managed to manhandle it into the runabout, we nearly had two sinking boats on our hands. It took some careful handling of the runabout to get the pump out to the sailboat.

Once started, the pump was so powerful that it sucked up everything that came within a foot of the suction line, but it had not come with a strainer. The result was that we had to clear the stalled pump of clothing and other personal belongings of the owner every few minutes. I tried to keep things away from the suction end, but soon discovered that, if I were to keep that up, the next thing that would have jammed the pump would have been my hand.

Eventually, we got down to the bilge and could see where the water had come from. A salt water intake hose for the forward head had decayed and given way. It was easy enough to close the seacock. It had been a long, hard struggle: working all afternoon, sloshing around in the flooded hull, cleaning out the jammed pump, working over the balky gasoline engine and, finally, tearing apart the whole boat to find the leak. But we had saved her and that made it all worthwhile. We put her back on her mooring, a wet, sodden mess, but still afloat.

Beverly wired her owner, who arrived in St. Lucia a few days later. "Dick the Twit", we called him. I never saw a more flamboyant style. He bounded aboard *Visitor*, full of exaggerated and hollow sounding thanks, and asked if there were anything he could do in return for my having helped salvage his boat. Well, I wasn't going to name a price. I didn't have

143

one in the first place; I had done what needed to be done. Secondly, I was irritated that he had asked. To my way of thinking, if you think someone has done something for you and you want to return the favor, you just do it: show up with a bottle of scotch, or an invitation to dinner, or whatever.

"No," I said. "I don't think there is anything you can do."

"OK. Well, thanks."

And that was the last I ever saw of Dick the Twit. He told Beverly to sell the boat, which she somehow did, several months later.

There was another poor, tired old boat, tied up on the other side of *Visitor IV*, that I saw slowly go to pieces during one year. I watched as her once proud varnish cracked and peeled and as her rigging frayed, rotted and finally broke. I saw her paint blister and peel, and her decks and hull planking dry out and separate. No one wanted her, least of all her owner, who hadn't even paid her dockage for many months.

One morning, I woke up to see her sitting on the bottom, with only her deckhouse and masts showing. Somehow, Ross and some of the Ganter's gang got her afloat, and then she was stripped of everything of value. People took the woodwork panels from her deckhouse, her wheel, navigation lights and other hardware. In a matter of days, she looked like a cadaver that had served too many medical students. We towed her out beyond the Harbor and gave her a decent burial, if nothing else. Old age was a hard thing to look upon and I often thought of her after she was gone. She was only a boat, but she had been my next-door neighbor for more than a year and, in her quiet way, a good friend.

We had another strange old schooner yacht, about 110 feet long, that had been tied up at the fuel dock before the schooner *Jylland* had arrived on the scene. A page out of history, this once grand ship had been made for a role in a movie and had never been constructed with the real craftsmanship and especially with the quality which would have normally gone into such a vessel. The years had been hard on her and

144

her absentee owners had been harder still. They never seemed to have the money so obviously needed to make extensive repairs. They were an older couple and, while they both had a will of iron, they simply didn't have the strength to go with it.

Her interior was dark, with handsome paneling of exotic woods, and there was worn and cracked leather upholstery on lounge chairs and built-in settees. Threadbare, stained Oriental rugs were scattered about on the floorboards, all a silent testimonial to better days, long since gone.

Her engine room was a shambles: an incoherent mess of wires, pipes, valves and machinery, covered with a thick coat of oil and grease. I was shocked when a St. Lucian taxi driver, that I had come to know, told me that, many years ago, he had been the engineer on board the schooner. In those days, he had kept a bright shine on the copper oil drip pan under the engine. He said that he had been aboard about a year ago and had cried when he had gone below into the engine room.

She was moved out on anchor, one day. There was a lot of controversy about why. The marina said that the insurance company didn't want the boat up against the fuel dock. Most of us suspected that it was because the bills had not been paid. Out there, she went from bad to worse. The woodworm damage at her water line was so severe, that you could see it clearly from a hundred feet away. Every morning, the fact that she was found afloat amazed us all.

One late afternoon, as I returned from a day charter and entered the Harbor, I saw the schooner on the far south end, about twenty feet away from the rocky shore. There was a one to two foot swell running, and I couldn't believe that she had not already begun to pound. I asked the charterers' indulgence while I went over to see what the trouble was. She had dragged her anchor over the deeper part of the Harbor and, just before reaching the rocks, the anchor had caught again on the bottom as it rose toward the southern shore. There was a gang of West Indians aboard, two authorized as watchmen by the owners during another of their visits to the United States, and a number of the watchmen's friends, unauthorized and enjoying the whole thing immensely. None were ca-

145

pable of operating the boat, but they were struggling with the giant deck engine, in hopes of getting the anchor up.

Now there is only one captain of a ship, whoever he may be and whatever his qualifications. He is in charge and no one else. But, I wanted to save that schooner, if I were able. I came alongside and asked for the captain. The head watchman appeared, with a worried look on his face. He was obviously out of his depth and had the common sense to know it. I asked him if he wanted help. He said he did, but didn't know what. He thought the most important thing was to get the deck engine running, so as to raise the anchor. I asked him what he would do to keep her off the rocks when the anchor cleared. He allowed as how he would start the main engine and power away. Did he know how to do that, I asked. He said no. About that time the deck engine came to life and the chain began to lift.

I suggested to the captain that I had best make *Visitor* fast to him, so that he would have power to get out of there, if he needed it. He agreed. With this official permission to get into the act, I had Placid rig every fender we had and most every line. I have never liked towing and much prefer to tie alongside, seas permitting. Then a fortunate thing happened: a great giant of a Welshman, Guy Neil by name, arrived on board, somehow, to see if he could help. Guy was the head of the construction crew that was working on the new harbor scheme and their major project, a massive new jetty, was three months ahead of schedule, due almost exclusively to the talents of one Guy Neil. I was glad to see him.

For one thing, not only did we have a balky deck engine, we had an engineering feat of no small magnitude ahead of us. The schooner had been out on anchor for some time, in fact, out on two anchors. The first halting work of the engine had brought up enough chain to expose fully the snarled mess the two chains were in. Of course, they went out through individual hawsepipes, but they were connected to the same windlass. Raise one and you raised the other. The clutch, which might have separated them, was rusted and forever wedded to its shaft.

146

By now, it had turned dark and I played my spotlight on the forward part of the schooner, where the work was going on. My charterers, incidently, were having a terrific time. I had offered to try to find a way to get them to shore, but they would have none of it. They wanted to watch the action.

Guy organized the crew, both authorized and unauthorized, into a work force not unlike one that he might have on his new dock. It wasn't long before he had the engine working and chain coming aboard. I could tell when she began to be free of the bottom and I applied power in firm, but judicious amounts, until we were clearly headed away from shore. It was slow going, but within a half hour, we had her back where she belonged. Guy let go the anchors and all the chain there was aboard to prevent a reoccurrence.

I went to bed that night happy at having been able to do something constructive again with my boat and my skills. There had been no brass band playing when I had gotten in, but a couple of my charterers had commented on how well it had worked out, which had pleased me.

But people are funny. I still get irritated at their behavior and do things I shouldn't. About three weeks later, the owners of the schooner returned to St. Lucia. Several weeks went by with them coming and going about the marina, trying to accomplish one thing and another concerning their old boat. They knew I had been instrumental in saving the thing from an early grave, because Beverly had related the whole tale to them. They never once stopped by to thank me. The more time that went by, the madder I became.

Finally, I got so mad, I typed out an invoice for services rendered at a cost of one hundred dollars and put it in their mailbox at the marina office. I got a check the following day in my mailbox. I still have it. I like to look at it occasionally and wonder what makes people tick.

I have had some long, questioning thoughts about people who operate yachts in the West Indies. Inconsiderate and discourteous boaters may be found anywhere, but my experience in the West Indies left me with the feeling that there was a

147

disproportionate number of them in those waters.

One skipper, however, shored up my faith considerably. A call for help had come over my telephone on board *Visitor*, one afternoon, from the manager of the little hotel at Anse Chastenet, the bay where *Visitor* stopped for swimming. There was a textbook reef just off the headland between Anse Chastenet and Soufriere Harbor. I often pointed it out to charterers, because it was such a classic example of what a reef looked like and showed clearly where it was safe to take a boat over and where it was not.

It first became visible from about a quarter of a mile away. It was necessary to come closer to see the classic color differentiation. The deep blue water changed to a light green, then to yellow and, finally, to dangerous brown. Generally, any but the very deep draft yachts can clear the yellow, but never, never should any boat try to cross a reef showing brown. There was plenty of brown on this reef, located about two hundred yards off the headland. Everyone knew it was there and we all had stayed clear of it, until that unfortunate afternoon.

The manager had called to tell me that a 110-foot schooner had run hard aground on the reef and had spent all day trying to get off. Would I come down and see if I could help? I took Placid off the work he was doing and we got under way within five minutes. It usually took an hour and a half to get to Soufriere on *Visitor*. We made it in one hour flat that afternoon.

She was hard on, there was no doubt about that. Eight to ten inches of her bottom paint was showing. I recognized her as a nearly new, steel hull beauty I had seen a number of times on other trips to St. Vincent and Grenada. Knowing she was steel removed some of the urgency, but she did have a list and was being moved and rocked by the swell. I came alongside as close as I dared and asked the skipper if I could help. He replied that he would very much like a pull. I backed away to give me sea room while I rigged a bridle. I knew my midship cleats were held by well-backed through bolts, so I made fast to the port cleat with an almost new piece of $\frac{3}{4}$" nylon. From there I led it along the deck aft to the stern, across the surface of the thwartship transom platform, or covering board, as it is sometimes called, to the starboard side, then forward to the starboard midship cleat. I left enough slack at the stern to facilitate bending on the towline. As I looked at my work, the only thing that bothered me was that, as the bridle would take the strain, it would form a vee that would bring pressure to bear on the upright corner posts which supported the cockpit hardtop. In an attempt to prevent this and to spread out the load, I made a bad mistake. I picked up the line where it lay next to each of the corner stern cleats and took one loose turn around their bases. I thought this would help to guide the bridle at the point where it left the stern, without putting too much strain on the stern cleats. I had not made the line fast by cleating it. My thought was that the stern cleats would take some of the strain, but would pass most of it through the turn to the midship cleats.

The schooner's dinghy brought us out the towline, which made things a lot easier. I bent it to the bridle and went up to the wheelhouse to square away for a tow. The idea was to pull her bow at a right angle, in an attempt to swing her. To do this to a wooden boat would be to risk twisting off a keel, but this was a steel hull, and the skipper had already had a crewman over the side to assess the problem from below the water. She was aground at the deepest part of her hull. Had only her bow been on, a tow astern would have made sense, but this was not the case. The skipper had tried everything during the morning. He had pumped bilges, pumped all the fresh water out, swung the boom, tried kedging off, using the dinghy to carry both anchors out. All to no avail. Even her tremendously powerful winches had not moved the anchor lines, only brought them so taut that there was real danger of them snapping.

I worked *Visitor* into the desired position and took up the slack. I ordered Placid out of the cockpit, in case the line should break. I kept a steady pull at 600 rpm for a minute or two. Nothing happened. I knew it would take more than that to budge the huge yacht. I moved the throttles up to 800 rpm and waited another two minutes. Still nothing. I went to 1000. My top rpm was 1800; *Visitor* cruised very nicely at

1500. I knew I was beginning to take a risk, but I hated to quit. I wanted to help and I wanted to get the job done. I went to 1200 rpm and I felt *Visitor* lurch forward. I immediately idled both engines and looked astern, expecting to see the schooner swing off the reef. Instead, I saw bits and pieces of my beloved *Visitor* flying through the air. There were white painted pieces and mahogany varnished pieces. I couldn't believe my eyes. And didn't want to.

Jumping from the wheelhouse, I ran for the cockpit. It was a mess. The thwartship platform which topped the transom had been pulled up into a vertical position from its normally horizontal one. The fold-down table, that should have been attached to it, was scattered all over the cockpit in splinters. I was staring at the underside of the platform with all its supporting beams, the inside of the transom planking, and the transom knee itself; all these things were seeing daylight for the first time in thirty years. Bits of coaming, toe rail and trim were everywhere. Most frightening of all, the top three transom planks had been pulled loose at their ends on the port side. Sick with apprehension, I ripped open the lazaret hatch to look for flooding. There was none. The transom was intact at the water line. When I realized there was no dangerous damage done, I again looked at the wreckage. I wept. I couldn't help it. That boat was everything I had at that point in my life, and I had put my heart and soul into it for almost two years. I loved it, but I had nearly destroyed it.

The explanation was simple enough. I was too new at my trade and the boat too old. The turn around the base of the stern cleats did not slip as the bridle tightened. It had caught and held, probably on both cleats. The strain had never been transferred to the strong midship cleats. With about eighty per cent of *Visitor*'s power on, the load had been too much for one set of cleats. Also, as later work on the damage was to show, there had been a fair amount of rot in the whole area. When the cleats had begun to come out, they had taken everything connected to them. What a mess it was.

Just at this time, the St. Lucia Police boat came on the scene. I had turned the towline free and the schooner crew

150

were taking it in. The skipper of the schooner asked me to come alongside so we could talk, but I could see that the police boat was coming in to help. I hollered over that I was OK for the moment and would stand by to see what the police would do. And what a performance they put on. They had a piece of line aboard that looked, from a distance, like 1¼" nylon. This they obviously preferred to use, rather than the schooner's line. It took everything the schooner's dinghy had just to tow it over to the stricken yacht. When the line was fastened, and it was a damn good thing it was well-fastened, the police boat did the most incredible thing I have ever seen done with a boat. The police boat was, if nothing else, of steel construction. While it may have been slow and cumbersome, it did have modern twin, V-8 diesel engines that, when they did work, were very powerful.

With my own eyes, I saw the boat reverse, while a police crew in the stern took in slack on the towline and flaked it on deck. With an estimated fifty to seventy-five feet aboard and the bitter end secured to some kind of bit or cleat, the skipper then clamped down full on the throttles. He had secured a running start. By the time the slack had run out, the boat must have been doing at least five or six knots, probably more. I was too mesmerized by the line to get a good estimate of the boat's speed. The line shot out of the water like a rod of steel. In a microsecond, it wrung itself dry, as spiraling circles of water flew from its core. Even from my position of perhaps two hundred yards away, I could see its diameter decrease. It seemed as though I could hear it sing, but I have been since told that was not possible. Watching it tighten, I could feel my body tense with it, until I thought that if the line didn't break, surely I would.

And then it moved. The bowsprit of the schooner began to move. And the bow moved. And the stern began to swing. She leaned over a little more. She was upright and free. Moving under tow and her own engine, which had been running full ahead the whole time, she rolled gracefully in the swell. A great cheer went up from on board.

The police boat simply took in their towline and, without

waiting to be thanked, began to return to Castries. The schooner and I maneuvered to within hailing distance.

"I'm going to take her to Marigot Bay for the night," her skipper called to me. "Can I come to see you at Ganter's about your damage, later on tonight?"

I was a little taken aback. This fellow had just freed his boat from a nasty grounding, but his immediate concern was when could he see me about my damage. Basically, my damage was my problem. I had offered to tow him of my own free will. It was my old boat and my bad judgment which had been the ultimate cause of the damage. I appreciated his concern, but called back that any time was all right. Didn't he want to see to his own boat first? He said that he was taking on no water, and that he would have to wait until morning light to check under water, anyway.

So, we separated, both heading north, he for Marigot and I for Castries. As I slunk into Vigie Creek, there was still enough daylight to make a full showing of the damage. By the time I had tied up and secured the engines, a small crowd had gathered to hear what had happened. They all came aboard for a closer look, as I explained the events of the afternoon. It was the most excitement we had had all month.

The gang of onlookers had polished off a bottle of Mt. Gay's finest before they began to drift off, but there were a few of the faithful still at the wake an hour later, when the skipper of the schooner arrived by taxi from Marigot. He must have called the taxi the minute he anchored. We opened a new bottle of Mt. Gay and went aft to survey the damage once again, only this time, it was because the schooner's skipper wanted a look. He went over it all very carefully.

"What do you think it will cost to put this all to right?" He seemed to be asking all of us.

We didn't know. We kicked it around; it really didn't seem as bad as it looked. The platform would have to be replaced, but ¾" marine plywood was available in Castries, so that would be no great problem. There would have to be a lot of cut and patch and some trim pieces would have to be handmade. It added up to a good week's work for a proper shipwright.

152

And there'd be some screws, varnish and paint needed.

"Do you all think three hundred dollars would cover it?" he asked.

It was almost as though he wanted a verdict from his peers. I hadn't said a word. My friends thought it over and agreed that it looked like three hundred dollars worth of damage, because labor costs in St. Lucia were a great deal smaller than those in Ft. Lauderdale. With that, he reached into his pocket and dug out a wad of bills. He peeled off three hundred dollars, shook my hand, thanked me time and again for my help, apologized all over the place for causing me so much trouble and disappeared in his taxi.

Although I was to see the boat many times afterwards I never saw him again. I often wondered if he were canned for running her aground or for being so generous with his owner's money. In fact, I never really did find out where the money came from. I did find out from him how the accident had happened, however, and it was another valuable lesson for me in boat handling. The schooner had been making a sweep inside Soufriere Harbor, so that the charterers could see the town. The water was very deep all around the Harbor, so it was possible to come very close to shore. He began to work out of the north end of the Harbor, knowing he would have to go well out to sea to clear the reef before heading up the coast to Marigot, his final destination for that day's cruising. At that point, he was tackled by a charterer who had been peppering him with questions all day. One of the charter captain's too many responsibilities was to keep the charterers happy at all costs, so he launched into an explanation of some fine point of sailing. Distracted from his work as helmsman, when he cleared the headland, he turned north. Within a minute, the schooner hit ground, while under power and at cruising speed. Lesson: when the captain is busy, he must tell the charterers to come back later. I occasionally had to suffer an indignant charterer, but I never felt very bad about it, after that. I also never went aground. Knock on wood.

Putting *Visitor* back together wasn't as bad as I had thought it would be. In fact, it was a very satisfying job. I did have

153

quite a time getting the piece of marine plywood from town to Ganter's, because I was required to buy a full-sized sheet. By the time it had been laid on my little dinghy, you couldn't see any part of the dinghy at all. Coming across the harbor, the boat looked like a 4 by 8 foot sheet of plywood, propelled by a Seagull outboard motor. With the plywood covering the entire boat, I was obliged to ride sitting on top of the plywood, in front of the motor. By the time I had tied up at Ganter's, I had the whole marina in stitches. I don't know why such beautiful wood was so readily available in a place like St. Lucia, but it was. The finish veneer was actually mahogany.

The first job was to refasten the transom planks. I removed the old fastenings and bunged their holes. Between the old holes, I drilled ones for the new fastenings. I then applied some polysulfide sealant to the edges and ends of the planks and began to draw them back into place with new fastenings. I was astonished by how neatly they fell into place. When all was tight and the excess sealant was removed, the bungs were in place and the whole area was sanded and primed, one would have never known that there had been any damage. It was fortunate that *Visitor* had a painted, rather than varnished, transom, however.

The rest of the job was to take several weeks of patient cut and patch. I began by doing the obvious. I tore out anything I didn't like the looks of and doused the rest with wood preservative. From then on, it was make a piece for here, make a piece for there, until the whole supporting beam area for the platform was rebuilt. I was able to use the damaged platform as a rough template to scribe the new piece on the plywood. It took several cuts and tries before the new platform fell into place. But when it did, the job seemed almost completed.

But there was still a lot of trim work to be done. It was a month later when I felt that I had built up enough layers of carefully sanded paint and varnish to finish the job. Of course, I was working on the project part-time. Once things were back together enough so that the charterers wouldn't feel the boat belonged in a shipyard, I only worked on it when there weren't more pressing things to be done. The little fold-down dining table had to wait some period of time before it was replaced with a magnificently finished piece of leftover marine plywood. I built it in the locker during my spare time, working up seven coats of varnish before I brought it out into the light of day. I remember carrying it past George on my way to *Visitor* to install it in the cockpit.

"Nice varnish, Mr. Bob. Nice varnish," he had said.

It was compliment enough for me, although many others were to bubble much more articulate praise.

The most involved rescue we had occurred shortly after I had completed work on *Visitor*'s stern. Everyone got into the act and it became a three-ring circus. It all began late one afternoon, when Bob Elliot picked up a faint call on his shore-based marine radio from Dan Flosac. Dan was lost. He had been returning from a trip to St. Vincent in his single-engine, 21-foot inboard-outboard boat. It was not an unusual trip. West Indian yachtsmen often braved the channels in boats that I would have preferred not to use for such a trip, and they always made it back, one way or another. Dan was a competent man, his boat was in good condition and he had one of the too few radios on the privately owned St. Lucian boats. He had with him several of his friends from St. Lucia.

Bob called me and asked if I wanted to go out with him to see if we couldn't track him down. We had him on the radio. Perhaps, if we went well off shore toward St. Vincent, we would see him. Dan had left the northern tip of St. Vincent with plenty of time to reach St. Lucia, but the visibility had been poor. We never had fog in the West Indies, but a distant rain squall could obscure land for a short period of time, and a kind of haze would sometimes do the same thing for the whole day. Dan had found himself in such a haze and hadn't been able to see the Pitons when he left the tip of St. Vincent. On a clear day, the Pitons were visible, so navigation was simply a matter of heading for them until you got there.

Dan knew how to navigate out of sight of land. Indeed, he had made the trip so many times, he knew the compass course and time by heart. So, he had settled down to his compass

155

and noted the time. He had put out a radio call, when he had estimated that he had run an hour more than would have been required to reach the Pitons. An hour in Dan's high-speed fiberglass boat was a long time. He said he was in fairly calm water, but could see no shore, and he was getting low on fuel.

What we needed was a radio direction finder. We had checked every boat in the anchorage for one before we had left, but to no avail. There were no RDF stations in those waters and no one would have relied on them if there were. But it was a shame not to have one now. We could have run Dan's signal down and brought him home in a few hours.

Bob and I looked up and down the coast about five miles offshore, until it began to get dark. We kept in touch with Dan by radio, but we couldn't find him. We even tried making an RDF out of Bob's boat by laying his antenna down on deck and rotating the boat to look for a null in Dan's signal. It seemed as though it should have worked, but we didn't get any readings that were consistent enough to be worth track-ing down.

By then, it looked as though we had another real problem on our hands. We had seen four people die during our fruitless searches and we'd be damned if it was going to happen again, particularly when we had these people alive and well on the radio. We decided to return to Castries and get organized. We found Beverly in her office, where she had been listening on her radio. She had informed the wives of the men about the situation and some of them were packed into Beverly's little office, listening to the radio as well. All they could hear was Bob's radio, because radio reception in the Harbor had always been poor.

Word had also gotten to the Hackshaw brothers, who were fueling up their boats. Bob went over to the fuel dock and filled his tanks as well. He then organized the boats into search areas based on the various calculations we could make for possible locations of Dan's lost boat. *Visitor IV* was as-signed to a location about two miles off the Harbor mouth to act as a radio coordinating base. I could talk with Beverly on

156

shore if that became necessary, and I could hear and talk to Dan better than most of the rescue boats. By the time we all steamed out of Castries Harbor, there were six of us. It was completely dark. The boats went to their areas and I established radio contact with Dan. His signal had become weak and I asked what was the problem. He had run out of gas, was drifting, and his battery was getting low. I suggested he keep his transmissions to a minimum to save power. He agreed, but he wanted first to tell me that someone aboard had found a flare. Just one? Only one. I alerted the other boats to this new development. We worked out an elaborate plan to station lookouts on each of the widespread rescue boats and, at my signal, Dan was to fire the flare. Just as we were ready, Dan came on the air.

"*Visitor IV*, this is Dan. I can't fire the flare."

"Dan, *Visitor*. What's the problem?"

"*Visitor*, this is Dan. It's not a flare. It's a yellow smoke."

Murphy's Law had struck again.

The radio silence that ensued for some time after that last transmission was broken by an astonishing call:

"*Visitor IV*, this is LIAT 475. Do you copy?"

LIAT was the Leeward Islands Air Transport Company, which amounted to the West Indies airline. It had a long and controversial history and was tolerated much the same way the telephone company was in the United States. It's all we had, so there wasn't much sense complaining. LIAT was nicknamed Leaves Island Any Time; it appeared to be a fair designation. Its problems were not caused by the pilots, who were as competent as any in the world. Somehow, I had one of them on the other end of my radio antenna. I discovered later that they often had the yachting frequency crystal in their radios, partly for something to listen to, and partly because they knew if they ever had to ditch, a charter yacht was the most likely rescue vessel. I recovered from my shock and pressed the mike button.

"Yah, LIAT 475, this is *Visitor IV*, loud and clear, over."

"Ah, *Visitor IV*, this is LIAT 475. Listen. I've been eavesdropping on you guys and maybe I can help. There is a limit to

157

what I can get away with, but here's my idea. First of all, I'm on the runway at Vigie. Now I don't have enough fuel aboard for a search and I'm about to take off on a scheduled flight anyway. But I can fly low over the area from the coast of St. Lucia to St. Vincent as I go south. If your lost boat hears me fly over him, have him give you a shout on the radio. You relay that to me and I'll give you my position. It'll be rough but it's better than anything you have now."

He was right on all points, so I accepted his offer and went through the tedious process of relaying the message to Dan and the other boats. I then asked for complete radio silence from all concerned so that Dan's call would be heard immediately. LIAT 475 came on and told me he was cleared to take off and to stand by. His twin-engine jet was off the end of the runway and passing over my head in seconds.

"Ah, Dan, this is *Visitor*. The LIAT jet is in the air."

"Roger, *Visitor*." Dan's radio was weaker than ever.

Five minutes, then ten went by.

"*Visitor IV*, this is Dan. I haven't heard the plane."

It didn't seem possible. I radioed the plane, told him that he hadn't been heard and thanked him from all of us for his help. Obviously, Dan was nowhere near where we and he had thought he had to be. That jet, passing low down the coast of the two islands and over the channel, must have made a sound which could have been heard for five miles on either side of his track.

I called Beverly on the radio and brought her up to date. She had heard enough of my transmissions to have a good idea of what had gone on. It turned out the then Premier of St. Lucia, The Honorable John Compton, had joined the group in Beverly's office and had been assuming a leadership role at the shore base by contacting everyone he could think of to help with the search. It was through his efforts that we were able to discover there was a French warship in the area. They had said they would enter the search. We all knew that with their electronic equipment such as radar and radio direction finders that they would make short work of finding Dan. With the Premier's concurrence, we weary amateurs turned the job over to

158

the professionals and returned to Castries.

It was past two in the morning, so I went to bed. But, still anxious over Dan, I woke early the next morning and called Beverly at her home to get the news. Dan had been located within two hours after the French Navy had gotten on the job. They had arrived at his location, some 50 miles due east off the coast of St. Lucia, about an hour later.

The French had given Dan a tow for about 30 miles, until he could see St. Lucia on the horizon. They had then transferred gasoline to him and had sent him on his way home. All of the rescue boats, except *Visitor IV* which was too slow to keep up with the small, high-speed jobs, dashed out of the Harbor to greet him. They met him about three miles off shore and, single file, formed a parade behind him as he headed on toward Castries Harbor. As they came in, everyone opened up to full speed. They made a wide swing around the Harbor and up to the customs and immigration dock where, lost at sea or not, Dan had to clear his boat and passengers into the port. John Compton was there, so port formalities were waved on the spot.

The parade formed again and powered into Vigie Creek to tie up. Weary as they were, the survivors were not going to miss the chance to tell their tale to the huge crowd that had gathered around Dan's boat. The question of the hour was: how had Dan gotten so far out to sea? Someone in the group, looking over Dan's boat, found the answer. By accident, the toolbox has been set down right next to the compass and no one on the boat had noticed it. When it was picked up and moved, we all watched the compass swing over 30 degrees to a new heading.

When I wasn't occupied with the chartering, the renovation work and the rescues, I sometimes amused myself by simply observing life. We certainly had some interesting specimens to observe. I don't know that we had any more or less than our share of the strange ones, but we were kept well-entertained by those we had.

During the time I was in the West Indies, I saw the most incredible young men and women whom at one time it was fashionable to call hippies, moving in and out on the damnedest, motliest boats imaginable. The boats had two things in common: they were powered by sail and they were a mess.

Their topsides were often painted many colors, if at all, or, if one color, always in desperate need of redoing. Rigging seemed in imminent danger of collapse. Masts were twisted and splitting. Varnish was obviously something to be avoided at all costs, and machinery in working condition was a testimony to the skill of the manufacturer, not to that of the current owner of the boat. Quite often, when a sailboat would come into the anchorage, the crew would swim ashore. They were unable to dock because the engine was inoperative and they had no dinghy. Some would arrive without even anchors and would sail about the anchorage, asking to be allowed to tie alongside an anchored yacht. Sails were often rags sewn together with bits and pieces of scrap canvas. Electrical components were always a great mystery to these strange ones. I sometimes came around to explain that batteries had caps so that water could be added, and that lacking water, a battery would die. Or, I would point out that an unsoldered electrical connection would not function when exposed to salt water spray. Safety equipment was usually nonexistent as were operable electronic systems. And yet the strange ones survived.

While the strange ones could be simplistically described as hippies, they had a strong, healthy look about them which separated them clearly from their land-bound counterparts in a way that could only be described as an improvement. But the long, dirty matted hair, the beards, the ragged clothes, if any, the carrying-the-burdens-of-the-world slouch were all there. The girls always looked too young and the men too old to be doing what they were doing. And both were always, in keeping with the standards of the culture, in desperate need of a bath.

Their spirits were unsinkable, if their boats were not, and most of the shortcomings of their boats were as much the result of simple lack of money as of lack of know-how. Few lacked the desire to learn and to do better as far as their boats and sailing were concerned. Many drove the more knowledgeable of us crazy with constant questions and occasional requests for help. One of the big chuckles of the week occurred when Roger Fothergill, an Englishman of dry wit and a lifetime of yachting skill, was overtaken on the dock at Ganter's by one of the strange ones.

"Ah, sir, do you know anything about compasses?" was the halting, timid question asked of Roger by a bearded wonder, clutching his sailboat's compass to his breast.

"I think I should recognize one should I see one," was the reply of a man who had crossed the Atlantic in his own yacht more times then he could remember. Being the true

162

yachtsman that he was, however, he spent the rest of the afternoon helping the young man to unravel the mysteries of a deviation table and its construction.

One of the strangest arrived by airplane, not by boat, and it was all Beverly's fault. Beverly had come to the conclusion that *Maid of Aaron,* home to her and son Craig for many years, had to go. She wanted a place of her own that was, if nothing else, on good old terra firma. So she announced, amid gales of laughter from all who heard her, that she was going to sell *Maid.* There were those among us who said that, if she were able to sell that floating derelict, they would buy her a steak dinner; they lived to eat that steak. Others, the more conservative among us, said simply that if Beverly were able to sell *Maid of Aaron,* she could sell anything. I am a living witness to the fact that Beverly can indeed sell anything, for sell her she did: not once, but twice, in the same year.

The first of Beverly's buyers for *Maid of Aaron* was a scrawny, bony, pasty-skinned hillbilly from Kentucky, one of those unfortunate males who could not raise a beard, but insisted on trying. Were he not a Caucasian, he could have been mistaken for Ho Chi Minh. I knew him, as did almost everyone else, only as Van. The most incredible fact about him was that he had never seen a boat or its customary habitat in his life. This helped to explain Beverly's success in selling, but hardly lessened the amazement we all felt. *Matron of Arron,* as some of us called her, needed everything. She hadn't even been hauled to have her bottom done in four years, an unheard-of thing there, the home of the woodworm. Her topsides had dried out to the point that daylight shone through the hull planks. She was double-ended, a sort of Colin Archer design, and all of the planks at the stern had pulled out of the stem. Rot was everywhere in the topsides and cabin wood. The engine had not been run in four years and was seized beyond repair.

Van came to ask me if I would survey the hull; I had been doing underwater hull surveys for the Lloyd's surveyor for some time. I told him there was so much growth on the hull

163

that I couldn't make any kind of survey. He insisted that I put on scuba gear and look at it anyway. I was furious at his stupidity, so I told him that it would cost him fifty dollars.(I usually charged twenty-five dollars for a quick check of the basics.) To my astonishment, he agreed. So, I put on the equipment, went down, swam the length of both sides of the hull, looking at the three-inch thick layer of marine growth, and came back to the surface. I told him the bottom was covered with growth and I couldn't see a thing. He paid me my fifty dollars and thanked me for my help.

It was a toss-up as to which was the greater of the two lost causes: the boat or the new owner. But Van was able to see some of his problems, and he went after them with a vengeance, if not with wisdom and skill. I saw him try to refasten loose planks with galvanized nails. He put two full gallons of automotive body putty into the open seams at the pointed stern. Then, thinking his structural problems were solved, he shocked the marina by painting the entire boat from the water line to the tip of the main mast with institutional green house paint. It was god-awful.

Word got around that Van was going to sail the beast to Martinique to have her slipped and her bottom cleaned and painted. By then, St. Lucia had lost her slipway to the Harbor project. We all tried to dissuade him from going, but what that lost soul lacked in experience was compensated by his pigheaded obstinacy. So, one day, Van was given a tow out to the mouth of the Harbor and turned loose into the hands of fate. Some of us actually thought we would never see him again.

But we did, four days later. He was being towed back by a fishing canoe with a 20-horsepower outboard. He had never gotten more than ten miles from St. Lucia. He put the green death back at her dock and left for the United States, in what can be best described as despair. Few of us felt very sorry for him. It was impossible to respect him because, while he was totally out of his depth, he didn't have the common sense to recognize it. It was impossible to help him because we all came to realize that he would drive us mad with a thousand unthinking questions which, in charity, we would make an effort to answer, then he would go his own way, completely ignoring all the advice. His manner was worse. He would drop right into the middle of a conversation with his problem of the moment and expect all to stop and listen. Most of us were glad to see him go. All of us were astonished to see him return two weeks later. This time, with an engine.

God knows where he had gotten it, or what its history had been. None of us could identify it, except we knew that it took gasoline and it was not a marine engine. He had asked everyone about a replacement engine before he had left and had been told that one could be found in St. Lucia with little trouble. In fact, the repair shop had had one which would have served well. True to form, he had ignored all the advice and had bought an engine in the U.S. He had had it shipped air freight to St. Lucia.

I had my suspicions about that engine from the moment I saw it, but kept them to myself. Van labored for weeks to get the old engine out and the new one in place. The concept of shaft alignment never occurred to him, until he tried to bolt the two shaft flanges together. Even then, it was no such fine point as alignment which troubled him, but rather the difference in the flange designs which made lining up the bolts impossible. He solved that problem by removing the two flanges with four days of backbreaking work and taking them to a machine shop to have them redrilled to match.

Finally, the whole mess was bolted together and in place. No attempt had been made to shim the engine to the vitally close tolerances required for the mating of the shaft couplings. The exhaust was a dry pipe that came out of the side of the hull through a hole he had cut. The cooling water came out through a similar hole and was carried in a piece of green garden hose. Van started the engine and it ran. Roughly, and with a lot of black smoke, but it did run. He then decided it was time for sea trials and, at once, cast off the lines and allowed the boat to drift away from the dock. He then put the monstrosity in what he thought was forward gear. Three things happened almost simultaneously. First, the propeller bit in hard, in reverse, and the stern was pulled sharply down

165

into the water. Second, there was a horrible noise inside the boat. Third, the engine died.

The long and short of it was that he had a wrong rotation engine with no gear reduction and no shaft alignment. The prop, turning in reverse rather than forward, tried to turn so fast that its load stalled the engine and at the same time broke the coupling into a hundred pieces.

Van's response was a little tragic. He threw over the anchor where he was and then sat down on the deck. He sat there for the rest of the afternoon without moving. In fact, by the time I went to bed, he was still sitting there on *Maid of Arron*, anchored in the middle of Vigie Creek. I suppose that he eventually went to bed. By the next morning, the boat was tied up at her dock and Van was gone. He wrote Beverly from the U.S. and asked her to sell the boat for what she could get.

Well, she did it again. To another bearded wonder, who also had never seen a boat or its natural habitat in his life. There was a significant difference, though. This fellow's ears were attached to his brain and there was an identifiable cause and effect relationship between advice given and action taken. He, too, worked long and hard on the old sailboat, trying to rectify the ravages of age as well as the mistakes that Van had made. It was a formidable task, but he kept at it until almost unbelievable things had been accomplished, not the least of which was the alignment of the engine. The lack of a reduction gear could not be solved properly without completely changing the engine. He did the next best thing; he changed the prop. He found a much smaller one and, after removing the shaft and having it turned down to a taper which would fit the smaller prop, reinstalled the whole thing. The prop turned at an incredible speed and was very inefficient, but at least it wouldn't stall the engine. The rotation problem was solved simply by getting used to pushing the shift lever forward to go in reverse and vice versa.

Eventually, he took *Maid* to Martinique to get her bottom done. He returned to St. Lucia to report that, unbelievably, there had been no worm damage of any serious consequence. No planks had had to be replaced and, in spite of a lot of re-

166

caulking, the hull was as sound as could have been expected and then some. It wasn't long after that that he left for Florida. Some months later, rumor had it that he had arrived there and had sold *Maid* at a substantial profit. Ya never know!

Some of the strange ones seemed to pride themselves in maximizing discomfort. I remember one infinitesimal yellow sailboat which simply appeared at the fuel dock one morning. It couldn't have been more than 18 feet long. It had a self-steering device, the wind vane of which was actually made from orange crate slats nailed to the end frames of the same crates. The counterweights were old scuba diving weights, lashed in place with twine. A talk with the boat's owner and skipper revealed that he had just come across the Atlantic from England and was on his way to Panama and the Pacific. The other two men aboard, he had picked up at his first land-fall, Barbados, and they were only going as far as Panama.

"After all," the singlehander said, "there isn't enough room aboard for the three of us on a really long cruise."

Then there was the 32-foot trimaran, which tied up next to me for a week. That cruising boat had aboard three adult couples and five children, ranging in age from six months to twelve years. There were also two dogs, three cats and enough bicycles to get most of them on wheels for shore excursions. I was invited aboard for a drink one night and, five years in the submarine service notwithstanding, I had to get outside after several minutes or I would have blown a fuse. How they survived at sea was totally beyond my reach, but they did. They had started in the United States and were on a trip down the entire chain of islands to Trinidad.

Among the strange ones were two Germans, who came into anchorage at the start of my second season. They were in their late 40s and looked like a pair of wild north woodsmen. Both had enormous beards, one flaming red and the other jet black. Neither could speak English very well, but we were all given to understand that the two of them had sailed their 48-foot boat from Bremen, Germany, and that they were broke and

167

wanted to do day chartering. I was not pleased at the thought of more competition, but they had a small sailboat and, from the looks of the two of them and their boat, I couldn't see much to worry about. They were as scroungey looking as any two self-respecting hippies and their boat was worse. They were inordinately proud of her; it seemed that Hitler had personally been aboard her to present a cup when she had won a race.

They had been in St. Lucia several weeks when one of the hotel managers stopped me in his lobby and asked to have a word.

"Do you know who those bearded German characters are?" he wanted to know.

I told him what little I knew about the two and asked why he was wondering about them.

"Bloody hell," he said. "I don't mind someone trying to make a few dollars, but these blokes are a bit much. I mean, they don't bathe in the first place, and they don't wash their clothes either. And they come around the guests at dinner and plead with them to go out on their boat. I was talking with a couple tonight who went with them. They said they didn't mind the dirty glasses the rum punch was served in. They just didn't drink it. But they did not like being lectured about how Hitler had been aboard, and about the rise of the Third Reich, and so on and so on."

"Hell, the war's been over for a long time," I said matter of factly. "What's the problem?"

"Well, old boy," he said, "the war isn't all that over for people with names like the Rosenbergs in room 207, and these chaps had better realize it."

They didn't last long, needless to say, and one morning I woke up to see their boat gone. I didn't miss them.

My classic strange one really didn't belong to the company of the incompetents. Orien Lindberg was as competent an individual as I have known. But he was a strange one, all the same. I never did find out what had brought Orien to St. Lucia, but he had been there for some time when I arrived. He

168

had married a St. Lucian girl and they had a cutie pie of a child. Orien was a Swede and still had a delightful accent. He was a young man, perhaps in his early thirties, too thin and too pale, but with boundless good spirit. He was always smiling, quite often prompting those like myself, who tended not to smile, to do so as well.

Orien's claim to fame was as a mechanic in general and as a refrigeration and air conditioning repairman in particular. He knew nothing about boats, but was often called to the marina to repair a yacht's refrigeration unit. He was also a scuba diver and, at the time, had the only air compressor on the island.

He was really a good sort and I have always hated the day that I had to read him the riot act. Orien's work was hot and dirty, which was an honorable estate. He had begun to get into the habit of stopping at my boat to socialize after completing a job in a yacht's greasy engine room. I was flattered that he wanted to stop by and chat so often, but I had put a lot of money and work into redoing *Visitor*'s interior and I just couldn't have grease and dirt on my upholstery and carpeting. To this requirement, Orien was totally oblivious. No amount of hinting would get the message across. He was one of those happy people who couldn't be insulted. No critical comment registered. So, one day, I simply had to tell Orien that I was glad to have his company, but he could not come aboard the boat. What I would have considered pure insult didn't phase Orien a bit. He came as often as before to chat and have a beer, sitting on the threshold of the salon door with his feet on the dock. I was always glad to see him.

Orien's fame as a mechanic was well-known, so when the owner of the *Wernadia* wanted to have that great hulk's monstrous engine rebuilt, Orien was the obvious candidate for the job. *Wernadia* was another of those large, ancient Baltic traders that had been taken out of honest work and converted to a gentler trade as a pleasure boat. She belonged to an American, whom I never met, although *Wernadia* had been there before I was and was there when I left. The American owner sold her to, but had not received payment from someone who had high hopes of making her into a floating scuba diving school. One of the many individuals I saw in St. Lucia whose reach exceeded his grasp, that man had made a down payment on the boat and then had insisted that he was going to take her out for a trial. He didn't have the foggiest notion of what he was about, especially concerning the operation of her huge, two cylinder, Swedish engine. There was a valve of some sort, which he failed to open. The engine simply blew up and the boat had to be towed back in. The buyer felt the whole thing was the owner's fault, refused to pay any more money, and eventually left St. Lucia and the boat. The owner went to court over it about the time I got there and, in the meantime, he wanted the engine repaired.

No one who saw the engine thought it could be repaired. One of the two cylinder heads had been broken into little pieces, bearings were gone, a rod was bent and the condition of the shaft was a mystery. Moreover, it was an obscure Swedish machine, the workings of which no one understood. No one, that was, except another Swede: Orien. To him, it was a labor of love, a return to the land of his birth, a chance to work with a fine piece of machinery.

Orien, we were later to discover, had a few aces up his sleeve. He had recognized a spare head among all the debris in the engine room, as well as other spare parts. He knew from experience how the engine worked. To him, it was just another repair job, but a long one. It almost seemed as though Orien had disappeared aboard the *Wernadia*. There would be days on end when no one would see him, but we could hear him banging away on something or other, deep in her engine room.

He did surface for a few days to rebabbitt the main bearings, a task demanding consummate skill and good light. We were all delighted that he elected to do it on deck, because we wanted to watch. It was an art that was little practiced. Orien had found spare Babbitt metal among the junk, as well as babbitting tools. He put on quite a demonstration, as he melted out the old metal and carefully cleaned the bearing shells. He then melted the fresh Babbitt metal and poured it in place. There followed several days of tedious trips down to the engine, where he pressed the bearings against their mating surfaces on the shaft, turned them back and forth, then brought them out into the light of day to look for the telltale, shiny high spots. These, Orien would gently stroke with a babbitting tool, until, in his judgment, they were gone. Then back to the shaft with the bearing shells for another try.

A month of almost daily work passed before Orien announced he had been painting the completed engine. It would be ready to start any day. "Yust a few more finishing touches," he would say. Clearly, there was to be no advance announcement and no audience at hand, when he finally charged the air start bottles and opened the start valve.

About this time, my father came to St. Lucia to visit me. He had an abiding love for boats, and I suspect I got a good deal of my fix-it skills from watching over his shoulder. I had a good time showing him my little bits of progress with *Visitor IV,* and it was nice to have an audience who recognized what I was trying to do and could appreciate it. We were sitting out in the cockpit after dinner, watching the day come to a peaceful end. We had eaten there on the little fold-down table and I still had a candle burning in a hurricane lamp.

Suddenly, the stillness was broken by a totally new sound. It was coming from the corner of the marina. I looked over to see what was going on. I realized the noise must be from an engine, but it sounded like no engine I had ever heard in the marina—a sort of pap, pap, pap, pap, with each sound having a hollow rap to it.

"The *Wernadia!*" I exclaimed to my mystified father. "My God, he did it! Orien got the damn thing running."

I spent a few minutes bringing my father up to date on what had been happening to the old boat. Then Orien came half running down my jetty, calling my name. He was covered with grease and sweat and was out of breath. I called out my congratulations, but he had no time for that.

"Do you have a chart of Martinique that I could borrow?" he asked.

"Yes, but what do you want that for?" I replied.

171

"I'm taking *Wernadia* to Martinique tonight to get her into the dry dock. There is a vacancy there, if I can get over right away, and the owner wants her dry-docked and her bottom painted."

"Orien," I asked, knowing the answer already, "what in hell do you know about taking a 90-foot boat to sea?"

"There is nothing so special about it. Besides I have flown to Martinique. I know what the harbor looks like from the air. That's enough. But a chart would help."

I tried to explain that there was a lot more to going to sea than recognizing the port when you saw it, and that handling a large, cumbersome boat like the *Wernadia* took considerable skill. "How do you know she will keep running? You need an eight-hour sea trial before you go anywhere. You need a radio, and *Wernadia* hasn't got one. You need to have your head examined." Nothing penetrated. He was going with or without a chart and, not wanting to be responsible for making matters worse, I gave him my chart. He set off in the direction of the *Wernadia*'s berth and disappeared into the night.

She was moored stern to the shore bank. A half dozen various cables and lines secured her to the trees and she had both of her bow anchors set. I knew that if he were determined to go, he would need some help on shore. He had two St. Lucian men from his refrigeration business on board. When I got close to the boat, I made an astonishing discovery: *Wernadia*'s mainmast was hollow steel and served as the exhaust pipe for the main engine. The nicest little smoke rings were pap, pap, papping out of the top of the mast.

Actually, we all had known that the mast was steel. We had had a laugh some months earlier, when the *Wernadia* had been officially impounded by her owner to prevent the tentative buyer from taking her out again. An old tradition provided that a writ had to be nailed to the mast of a ship not cleared to leave the port, so that port officials could see it and prevent it from sailing. A very dignified St. Lucian customs officer had shown up at Ganter's one day with the writ and his hammer and nails. He had bent every one of the nails against the steel mast, before he had given up in disgust and

172

sought out some tape.

Orien and his men were laboring over the antiquated deck engine. It came to life as I arrived on shore, near *Wernadia*'s stern lines. They worked for some time to free the confused anchor chains and, on a signal from Orien, I let go, one at a time, the stern lines. Then, he must have put the engine in gear, because its exhaust note changed considerably and there was a splash of water under the stern.

Old *Wernadia* began to move forward for the first time in more than a year. I walked to the fuel dock to get a better view of her as she started to enter the anchorage area. There were a lot of yachts at anchor and I know Orien had his work cut out for him there. By now, there were eight to ten of us onlookers, and one of the crowd uttered a quiet, "Oh, my God." I looked into the darkness. Yes, there was going to be trouble. There was a lovely little white sloop and *Wernadia* was headed right for her. The exhaust pitch changed again, as Orien shifted into reverse, and *Wernadia* began to turn, but not enough. Her bow gave the little sailboat a glancing blow and brushed it aside. No real damage had been done. The sailboat just swung away on her anchor with a little Baltic paint on her side.

Wernadia was in full reverse and picking up speed. She was backing into Vigie Creek and showed no indication of stopping her reverse direction. As she came closer to the piers at Ganter's, I realized the great beast was headed right for my *Visitor*. I watched for a few terrified seconds to evaluate her sternward course. There was no question about it. *Wernadia* was out of control, in reverse, and making about four knots right for the stern quarter of my boat. I suddenly realized my aging father was still in the cockpit. I broke into a run, boarded *Visitor* with a leap and lurched aft to the cockpit. In a state of panic, I got my astonished father to his feet and began to push him forward to the salon. Seeing the burning candle in its hurricane lamp and thinking the anticipated collision might cause a fire, I threw it into the water. I had gotten my father on the dock and was heading shoreward, when the pap, pap, pap, pap of *Wernadia* seemed suddenly to be breathing

173

down my back. I turned to see what would happen.

Wernadia's side cleared my port stern quarter by twelve inches. As she passed, the clinker-built dinghy, hanging in its davits, began to meet the bow of the 45-foot sportfisherman that was tied up, stern to, on the other side of my dock. With a sickening crunch, the dinghy was impaled on the fishing boat's bow and rail and collapsed into splinters. The fishing boat's nylon mooring lines went as tight as steel. Her cleats pulled out of the fiberglass hull and flew through the air. The mooring lines snapped back like rubber bands, slamming the fishing boat's stern hard against the cement retaining wall that carried all the docks. As quickly as she had reversed into the fishing boat, *Wernadia* began to move ahead. The grinding, crunching noise was repeated as the wrecked dinghy disentangled itself from the bow rail of the fishing boat. The *Wernadia* had become a demon, hellbent on destroying anything in its path. It charged ahead as though it wanted to smash the Coal Pot restaurant. But the Coal Pot was protected by sandy shoal water, so the mad beast only succeeded in running herself aground. Her engine still panted in a wild fury and her propeller frantically thrashed the water. I saw Orien leap into the engine room hatchway and disappear. Seconds later, the tip of the main mast, which was also the exhaust pipe tip, began to blast forth hellfire. Sparks shot more than 50 feet into the air, followed by a ball of flame.

I was sure the engine was exploding. I jumped up and down on the dock, screaming, "Orien's down there! Get him out of the engine room!" Just then, there was an audible sign from the exhaust pipe, and, with a quiet puff of smoke, the engine died. There was complete silence.

The first person to break the silence was in the crowd with me. All he said was, very quietly, "Thank Christ."

Some of us rounded up a dinghy with an outboard and went to work rigging warps from *Wernadia* to the fuel dock. It took several hours of work, but we were finally able to free her from the sand and get her along the fuel dock. We also tied up the fishing boat and notified the hotel, to which she belonged, about the damage. After everything was secured, Orien left his "command" and ventured ashore as far as the fuel dock. It was difficult to ask him any questions. He had all the problems he could handle, and no one wanted to make it any worse. But we were really interested to know if he had any explanation for the boat's berserk behavior. Finally, someone asked what had happened. Orien had had a little time to think about it, and he knew one thing none of us knew. *Wernadia* had no reverse gear. Like the *Jylland*, she reversed by changing the pitch of her propeller. Her prop had not been pitched for a long time. The barnacles and the growth around the gear mechanism and the blades must have been tremendous. When Orien tried to reverse the pitch as he neared the little sloop, it had taken an enormous effort at the control wheel, hence the delay. Once pitched in reverse, the damn thing wouldn't come out. The tremendous load on the gears and the clutch froze them as well. Finally, after backing into the fishing boat, Orien had been able to repitch the prop forward, but had not been quick enough with the helm to avoid going aground. That was probably just as well.

All the sparks and flame from the exhaust pipe mast had been caused by a simple stack fire, a common occurrence when carbon has built up over the years. I knew nothing of such things, so my panic and fears for Orien's life had been groundless. He had simply gone below to shut the engine off.

The next morning, there was an unduly officious inspection of the fishing boat by the hotel people, who knew nothing about boats and succeeded only in making that painfully obvious. The skipper arrived later, a real professional from the Bahamas named Ted Knowles. He asked me to check underwater for damage to the props, rudders, and so on. It was hard to believe, considering that she had been pushed up against the retaining wall, but there was no underwater damage. The fishing boat's injuries were limited to three, torn out and missing cleats, a mangled bow rail and a little damage to the fiberglass at the point of the bow. The hotel management were clearly disappointed.

The *Wernadia* survived. Orien worked on the propeller with his diving gear and eventually did get her to Martinique for dry-docking. She was later sold to a group of American strange ones, who tried to make a living with her by carrying cargo from island to island. They seemed to survive at it and showed up in St. Lucia from time to time. But after two years, word got out that they were having trouble both as a group and financially. Bob Elliott, who had had enough of watching others make money with day chartering, thought he would give it a try and offered a low price for *Wernadia*. It was accepted. The *Wernadia* was one bit of competition too much and was one of the many things which prompted me to decide that it was, once again, time for a change.

There were a lot of things that went into my decision to leave. Most of them were intangible. After I sold *Visitor IV* and returned to the U.S., I was besieged by friends and acquaintances, even relatives, who would all ask, "Why did you give it up? You must be crazy!" In many ways, they were right. Having my own business and doing what I enjoyed most in life was a wonderful thing. There were exciting times during my three years in the West Indies, times that could never be duplicated within the confines of the usual, orderly life. It isn't every day that you get rammed by a 130-foot schooner! Those are the things that I still miss: the excitement, the variety, but most of all, the satisfaction and personal pride that comes from doing what you want to do and doing it well. I wish I had all those things now.

But there was a lot more to the experience than just the good things. There was, for example, that horrible disease, which mainlanders often got, called "island fever". It came on slowly and subtly. The first time it had hit me was when a friend had offered to loan me his little mini-moke car for the day. "Take it for a drive," he said. I had thought about it for a while and had realized there was no place on the Island that I hadn't been to by car too many times, so I had thanked him, but declined.

I began to feel it when I found that I didn't bother to pick up the menus in the restaurants. There were only three or four places that were fit to eat in, and I knew each of the menus by heart. I would order the same thing I had been ordering for months. Eventually, when I walked into a favorite place, the waitress, whom I knew by her first name, would bring just what I wanted, without being asked.

There were days when I would have liked just to be alone, to get lost in the crowd. It was impossible in a small place like St. Lucia. Going downtown was like going to a class reunion. If I were to sit alone in a corner of a restaurant, people would come up to ask if I were all right. If I were to park by the side of a deserted road for a chance to think, a good friend would happen by and offer to help fix whatever was wrong with the car. If I were to close up the boat, turn the air conditioning and the high fi on, someone would come to the window, wanting help with some electrical problem on his boat.

Normally, all these things were fine. But, I needed personal privacy, as well as people. It came at a high price, if at all, for an expatriate on a small island. The need for it and the lack of it contributed to island fever.

Another hazard was that, when there was nothing to do, there was nothing to do. There was little or no television. Programs were rebroadcast from Barbados, so reception was poor and the programs were worse. The movie theaters were uninhabitable. Once, in desperation, I decided to go to the movies and mentioned it to Placid.

"Yes, Mr. Bob. But you doesn't be forget to wear your shoes," he said.

Footwear in that part of the world was usually open, rubber flip-flops, so I asked him why these wouldn't do.

"Does be rats, Mr. Bob, and dey does sometimes bite."

Feeling that perhaps he had discouraged me a little, he went on to point out with pride that I should be sure to get a first class ticket, because the first class seats had a fan for every four people. That was all I had needed to hear to keep me out of the movie houses forever.

A lot of expatriates spent their leisure time in the hotels, but this was no solace for me. The hotels were where I had to hustle, so I found going into them little more than a busman's holiday. Most were so badly managed that it was frustrating as well. At a place to get away from it all, you shouldn't have to beg for a drink at the bar.

I found myself spending most of my evenings and spare time aboard *Visitor*. I read an average of three paperback books a week during the off season. I doubt that I had read three books in three years, before I had come to St. Lucia. In the evenings, I did enjoy listening to music on my high fi, but, as island fever came on stronger and stronger, I found myself drinking more Mt. Gay Rum than listening to music. That was another bad sign.

Social isolation contributed to island fever. The clannishness of the expatriate groups limited my social life to the boating community, but during the off season there were few of us. Most of us knew each other too well and lived too close together, as it was. I tried to have outings on *Visitor*, where everyone would bring something and we would go to one of the little bays down the coast for the day. Bob Elliot and Mike Atkinson did the same with their boats, and it helped. Still, it was difficult to adjust to the lack of contact with people who were real friends, rather than just cohorts, all in the same bag.

None of this was really much of a problem during the tourist season, December to May, because the work kept everyone busy. Island fever was an off season malady that could strike with devastating results.

My restoration work on *Visitor IV* was virtually completed. The day I found myself carpeting the engine room, I knew I had reached a signpost. There was always work to be done. There always is, on any boat, or it isn't a boat, by definition.

179

But the work left was just routine maintenance, and there wasn't as much fun in that, as there was in yanking out two bushels of worthless wire from the engine room.

The competition was getting hotter. The *Jylland* was still taking the large groups. Bob Elliot's purchase of the *Wernadia*, while more of a problem to the *Jylland* than to me, was just another indication that perhaps my time had come.

Another contributing factor was that I had reached the point where I had been doing the same thing for too long a time. The charterers were wearing me thin. I found I didn't have the patience I once had with them. It was growing harder and harder to cope with their whims and fancies. I was becoming irritable and it was showing. To me, the worst part was that it meant I wasn't doing as good a job as I wanted to be doing. I was getting sloppy. I wasn't doing it right, so I began to think that the time had come, once again, for me not to do it at all.

One day, when things were slow, I trudged down to Beverly's office. My heart wasn't in it, but I knew it had to be done. It would probably take six months to find a suitable buyer, get the deal consummated and check him out on the operation of the boat. I had already made up my mind that I would include in the sale at least one week of my time with the buyer before he took over completely. If I were to get out of St. Lucia before the next off season, which I wanted desperately to do, I had to get started.

Beverly's office had always been a sanctuary for me. I kidded her that the only reason I stopped by was to soak up a little air conditioning. She had two of the biggest air conditioners on the island in her very small office. It was always lovely and cool in there. I spent a lot of time at Carib Cruises, and there were those who got their jollies from thinking that Beverly and I had something going together. Nothing could have been further from the truth. For one thing, we both had better taste than that. For another, we were too much alike to get along on any basis other than the quasi-business one we had. I would come in, plunk myself down in a chair, and we would talk boats and chartering and people for hours on end. When one of us got tired of talking, there was always the excuse of other work to be done.

We enjoyed each other. It was fun to compare notes to see who could make the best assessment of who would do what fool thing next. We were both good at repartee. While much of the banter sounded like school kids playing in the backyard, Beverly and I enlivened each other's dull days and, in a too small community of friends, it meant a lot to me. And she made a fantastic pumpkin soup.

I plopped myself down in a chair, without my usual cheery greeting. Beverly went on with her work, not looking up.

Finally, she said, "How much are you going to ask?"

"Ask for what?" I replied.

"For *Visitor IV*, dummy. What else?"

"What the hell makes you think I'm ready to sell?" I asked.

"Looked at your face in the mirror lately?"

"Smartass."

"And besides, it's time you got out of here. You've known it for a long time, and so have a lot of other people, including me. Besides, I need the commission on the sale."

"My friend, Beverly Pringle. Whatever would I do without you?"

We bantered about as usual, poking good fun at each other, but at the same time getting down to the sale of *Visitor IV*. We agreed on a price that would cover all the debts I had run up over the years, the outstanding balance on the bank loan, Beverly's commission and still leave something to help me start again in the U.S. Beverly agreed to advertise in several boating publications, including, obviously, the one she had used to find me two and a half years ago.

I went back to *Visitor*, feeling like the traitor I was, and sat down at the desk in my stateroom to write up some specification sheets. One of the things that had irritated me during many years of boat buying was the sketchy, inaccurate and contradictory information supplied by the seller. I was going to approach the sale of *Visitor IV* the same way I had everything else about her: do it right or not at all.

I dug out the old surveys, all four of them, and compared the

181

specifications. No one of them was accurate in such simple basics as draft, which varied from 3½ feet to 6 feet, and beam, which varied from 12 feet to 15½ feet. I had measured *Visitor*'s draft when she was on the slipway and had checked her length and beam with a tape measure when I was considering buying her. So, I began my listing with the correct dimensions.

I then went on to write out a brief, but complete and honest description of each compartment from the forecastle to the cockpit and wheelhouse. That took a typewritten page.

I then listed her equipment, including the auxiliary things in the engine room; ground tackle; electrical, electronic, and safety apparatus; and miscellaneous. I described the locker and its contents. All that filled a second page.

I put together a page about *Visitor*'s history, including what I had found out from Tom Vickery, two years ago at PSV. I brought her history up to date by detailing the major work I had accomplished during the past two and a half years.

Then, I wrote down everything I could think of about the business, including the number of hotels, the tourist bureau figures on tourism, the competition *Visitor* faced and some basic information on how my business had fared. That took another page.

Realizing that the average prospective buyer would know little about St. Lucia, or the problems and assets of living and working in the West Indies aboard a yacht, I put together another page on that subject. How I would have liked to have had that collection of information available to me when I had bought *Visitor*. When it was completed, it presented a clear and complete picture of what was for sale.

In fact, it looked so good, that I decided to go first class. I borrowed a friend's camera that had a wide-angle lens and took color photographs of the wheelhouse, the salon, my stateroom and the galley. I sent the film to the U.S. for processing and had twenty-five prints made of each of the pictures. I was able to buy 25 clear plastic, 8½ by 11 inch envelopes, punched with three holes, and, when my prints arrived, I mounted them in sets of four on sheets of paper. These, I put into the plastic envelopes. I then got twenty-five orange Duo-Tang folders with pockets built into the front and back covers. I had a printer in Castries type up my information sheets and print twenty-five copies of each. And I had the same number of photocopies made of my latest survey. I sorted them and put one of each into every orange folder with a copy of my brochure, a copy of the postcard photograph of *Visitor IV*, that I had always included inside the brochure, and a copy of the tourist bureau's brochure on St. Lucia. It was one hell of a package. No one has ever had a better reason to pay the sub-stanial air fare to St. Lucia than someone who received that folder.

My only mistake was that I should have made up at least a hundred of them. I couldn't have afforded it; the twenty-five cost more than one hundred dollars. But the response to Beverly's advertisement was nothing short of phenomenal. She ran a 3 by 5 inch ad with a photograph in a monthly boating publication and a similar ad in a magazine that catered more to commercial boating interests. Within one month, she received 97 letters, 13 overseas telephone calls and 9 cables. The boat was sold then, so we stopped keeping count, but the requests for information continued to come in for three more months. Beverly had to have a "sorry, you are too late" letter printed to meet the demand. Judging by the response, a lot of people wanted O-U-T in the worst way. And many of them thought that chartering a boat in the West Indies was the best way.

Many of the letters were from lawyers who represented clients whose names they were not about to divulge. Several of them flew to St. Lucia without bothering to write or make an appointment. They just showed up at Beverly's office, suit, tie, attaché case and all and asked for more information "for their client". They could have only been representing individuals of wealth, power and prestige, who wanted to be able to flirt with the idea of escape without the word getting out.

Other inquiries were from potential investors, who thought, because we hadn't given a price in the ad, that my little operation was a large moneymaking venture. We had no trouble explaining the facts of life to them, although one group did keep us busy. They were undaunted by the smallness of what I had for sale and insisted on coming to St. Lucia. There were four of them who came and they spent a week investigating all kinds of business prospects in St. Lucia. They were determined to find something to invest in, but they never did find what they wanted, so they finally left.

The serious inquirers, whom we felt would make good owners for *Visitor*, received the folder. They had all been sent out in two weeks. Beverly and I were a little choosy about whom we answered. Beverly would have to live in daily contact with the buyer and have regular business dealings. In other words, he would be another Ganter's expatriate. I would have to break the person into the business, introduce him to my contacts at the hotels and probably show him how to run *Visitor*.

Aside from the businessmen and the lawyers, whose interests were misguided, there were seven or eight potential buyers, some accompanied by their wives, who came to St. Lucia to see *Visitor IV*. They had only two things in common: they were almost all in their fifties, and they were making plans for their retirement years. Day chartering in the Caribbean was a reasonable choice for them. I would have recommended it to any retiree who had the cash to afford it and who had the health to do the work.

For most of those who came with their wives, it was clearly the women who couldn't bring themselves to accept it. The men were all hot to buy, but mama wanted more room for "her things" than there was on a 57-foot boat. My heart really went out to one individual who was in his late forties and recently divorced. He and his ex-wife had run a family business that he did not want to keep after she had left. He wanted to start from scratch on something totally new and different. How he agonized over his decision. He loved *Visitor IV* with a passion. He loved the island. He had the money in the bank. But he just couldn't bring himself to make a decision. He asked me to come over to his hotel one evening to talk some more. We kicked it around at the bar over half a dozen drinks,

184

until he was in tears from frustration. He was accustomed to being in business for himself and to taking the risks, which I had not been. That part of the decision was no problem for him. The thing that was killing him, oddly enough, was the part that had been the easiest for me. He had lived all his adult life in the same place, doing the same thing, and he couldn't make the break. I told him to go home and think about it. He did and wrote later that he had decided to stay put.

I was delighted that there was so much interest in the boat. I had been afraid that I wouldn't be able to sell it. Now, it looked as though I would have to beat off the potential buyers with a stick. It was trying work, explaining everything over and over to those who came to St. Lucia. I was getting weary of the "Professional Boat Buyer", who would try to poke every plank with an ice pick. He would complain about everything that was normal for a boat of *Visitor*'s age, yet say nothing about the one of two things that he might have reasonably questioned. Most of those who came to St. Lucia had precious little experience with boats, so even the most obvious things had to be explained in tedious detail, not once, but several times.

I was a little less than my usual jolly old self one afternoon when I returned from running an errand in town to find another total stranger and his wife actually aboard my boat, poking around. I asked him, in a tone that was less than sunshine bright, what the hell he was doing aboard my boat. He introduced himself as Dan Harrington. Didn't I remember his letter? Well, there had been a lot of them, so no, I didn't, but that was my fault and not his. By now, having had a look at him and his wife, I realised that coming aboard my boat without having been invited was not his fault either. They were clearly from rural somewhere, and most likely, were ignorant about boating courtesy.

He wanted to get right down to looking over *Visitor*, but I was hot and hungry and a bit put out at this guy, even if it wasn't his fault. Besides, I wanted Beverly to earn her commission, so I sent him to see her, which he should have done in the first place.

Dan Harrington was about the last person in the world I would have taken for a boat buyer. He knew nothing about boats or the water, but he somehow had gotten it in his head that buying *Visitor IV* was his life's ambition. No matter how hard he looked at her, he could find nothing to complain about. I personally didn't care whether he bought or not, but I was not looking forward to teaching him how to run a 57-foot boat when his experience had been limited to paddle boats in his local amusement park.

The thing which bothered me most about Dan was that he knew so little about boats that he couldn't and didn't ask any questions about *Visitor*. He offered to buy without even looking inside the engine room. He didn't ask to see any business records and showed no interest in looking around the Island.

Moreover, I couldn't see Dan and his wife as charter boat operators. They were both as nice as two people could be, but they were also just as colorless. The tourist trade, among a lot of other worthless things, takes a bit of the old pizzazz, of kidding around, of backslapping, of hustling. You have to look and dress the part as well. Dan and his good wife had none of these less than sterling qualities. Without them, not only was I afraid he would be unsuccessful, but worse, he would never understand why and his lack of comprehension might drive him to despair. He probably had been a success in his country life and proud of it, but I could only see him doomed to failure in this particular venture.

However, Dan was not going to be stopped. He had brought five thousand dollars with him as a down payment. He wanted to sign an agreement, then get back to his rural Canadian town and put his house up for sale to finance the rest of the price. Beverly and I were sick. She fully agreed with me that Dan was making the mistake of his life. She knew the area in Canada where Dan lived and described him as being what Americans used to call a country bumpkin.

We decided Dan needed protection from himself. With the help of a local barrister, we drew up a conditional sales agreement that no one in his right mind would have signed. It recognized the five thousand dollars as a nonrefundable deposit and included, in plain English, a clause which stated that, should a second offer to buy for immediate cash be made, Dan had 72 hours to exercise his option to purchase in full or forfeit his deposit. Living in Canada, it would take 72 hours just to wire the money, if he had it on hand, which he didn't. He was going to sell his house to get the money.

Dan signed on the dotted line and Beverly and I went down to *Visitor* and had three double rum and Cokes, without saying a word to each other. *Visitor IV* was as good as sold, and to the wrong guy.

Dan and his wife left on the afternoon flight. On that same flight, Dan's savior arrived. There hadn't been time to notify Alex Harkness of Dan's offer to buy, because Alex had been on his way when the offer had been made. Beverly met Alex and told him the boat had a first refusal offer, bound by five thousand dollars. Alex was a tall, athletic-looking guy, well-dressed and obviously on his toes. He had a million-dollar smile and an honest face. His response to Beverly's news was, "Well, let's have a look anyway."

Alex and I went over *Visitor* with a fine-tooth comb. He asked sensible questions about the boat and the business. The next day, he went around on his own to the various hotels and checked out the boat's reputation. He also, we found out later, talked to some key people in town about Beverly and me.

Within 48 hours, we had our second offer to buy for cash. It fell to Beverly to tell Dan. I wasn't there when she called and I'm glad I wasn't. She told me about it later.

"It was awful, Bob. He pleaded with me for a little more time. He offered to pay an additional five thousand dollars over our asking price. Bob, it was just awful . . . the sound of his voice. Finally, he broke down and cried. He wanted the boat that bad."

Beverly and I had agreed that we would not hold him to the nonforfeiture clause and she returned his deposit check. It seemed the only thing to do. And he said over the phone to Beverly that he appreciated that.

187

It's funny about Dan Harrington. Beverly and I still think we did the right thing. I even get a Christmas card from him every year, but I wonder if he ever understood.

Beverly and I were pleased with our new owner. Alex was all charm and personality. He was capable and quick to learn the intricacies of operating *Visitor*. Also, he could afford to own her without depending on chartering to pay all her bills.

Alex didn't want to take possession until June, which was fine with me. I could make a little money during the tourist season, then get out of St. Lucia at the start of the boring off season. He did stay for a week to learn the ropes, however.

Alex was not totally new to boats. He had a 28-footer of his own, so he had some idea of the basics of boat operation, for which I was thankful. We spent about two days going over *Visitor*'s machinery and equipment and we had a rundown of what was on hand in the locker. It was mostly me talking and Alex listening, but he was a good listener. When he interrupted with a question, it was a good one. We got along beautifully, something of a rarity between a new owner and an old owner, who was turning over his pride and joy.

We also spent a few days going around to the various hotels and meeting those managers who were, in my opinion, worth meeting. Some of the hotels played musical chairs with their managers, replacing one incompetent with another, no doubt with the hope that any change was better than no change at all. Those were the hotels from which I rarely had any cooperation or business, as I explained to Alex. Some of the smaller, privately-owned ones, such as East Winds, run by Margaret and Dick Egerer; Marigot des Roseau, owned by Joe and Emily Parlor; Terry and Walter Boudreau's Yacht Haven and Pat and Roger Hedley's Top of the Morne, were a joy to visit with Alex, because the owners were fine people and had always been helpful to me, even when I had been a neophyte. They were obviously ready and willing to do the same for Alex.

Getting acquainted with the managers of the large hotels operated by chains was a waste of time, but, over the years, I had established friendships with members of the staffs, who

188

were helpful. I also had working relationships with some of the water sports concessionaires, who, when faced with large groups they couldn't handle, would send business my way, for a commission. These were all informal arrangements, however, and often depended more on the personal relationship than the commission involved.

I had a new crewman named Andrew, the best of the lot. Placid and I had had a falling-out over the same thing that had caused me to fire some of my other crewmen. He had simply lost interest in the work and, rather than quit, had become impossible to deal with, until I finally had had to can him. It was a simple way to ensure getting some severance pay. If they were to quit, they would get nothing; if you were to fire them, you would be duty-bound to give them a week or two of pay.

I had a long talk with Andrew, explaining to him that the boat had been sold. I told him that it would be doing much the same work it had been under my ownership and that the new owner was a fine fellow. I told him that he was free to do whatever he wanted, but he should know that I had recommended him highly to the new owner and that Alex wanted him to stay. Alex would have been a fool not to; Andrew knew more about the boat than he did. Andrew seemed a little hesitant, but I finally got him to agree to stay with Alex for at least a season.

Finally, there was nothing to do but get Alex checked out on the operation of *Visitor* herself. He had been over the controls and not only knew what they did, but why, as well. I had shown him where the huge mechanical shifting rods came into the engine room and were linked with the transmissions. He knew that the start switches only energized the starter motors, because diesels have no electrical ignition system. He knew how to shut the engines down using the throttle shutoff and I had showed him the diesel emergency shutdowns. There was only one way to learn how to handle a big boat, I had told Alex, and that was to climb up into the wheelhouse and run it. I had tipped Andrew off that, while Alex's first attempt might be a little trying, he should remember how patient I had been with him during his first days working on board *Visitor* and he should do everything he could with line handling to help Alex.

Alex and I went up into the wheelhouse. He stood there staring at the controls as though he were face-to-face with his maker.

"Well, Alex, kick a tire, light a fire!" said I, remembering the exuberant cry of the helicopter pilots who used to fly me around Vietnam, when I was a news correspondent there.

"You mean, I should start the engines," Alex replied, looking at me as though I were his executioner asking him to pull his own switch.

"Fire 'em up," I said.

Alex pressed one of my nice new red start buttons and my starboard 6-71 jumped into life. That quick and faithful start had meant so much to me for nearly three years. I realized, at that moment, that I had lost my boat. No one but I had ever pushed those buttons. Not once. Until now.

He started the other engine and we let them run until the temperature gauges began to come up.

"What now?" Alex asked.

"Try your shift levers, one at a time, forward and reverse, to make sure they work. That way, the day after you have been working in the engine room and have forgotten to reconnect one of the levers, you will remember it while you are still tied to the dock."

He grabbed the port lever and gave it a tentative pull.

"Snap it back, Alex," I told him.

He did and damn near went on his backside, when it locked into gear.

"Pop it out," said I.

We tried out the gears a number of times and it wasn't long before Alex understood the technique of moving those levers. It was a difficult thing to explain; he just had to try it. I had him check out the throttles, as well, to make sure they were working smoothly and then said:

"OK, old man, you're all ready to back her out."

Andrew had been watching us closely. When Alex turned to

Andrew and told him to start taking in the lines, Andrew stood his ground.

"I must be doing something wrong," said Alex.

"De power line and de telephone, Mr. Alex," said Andrew.

Alex was a little taken aback, but I never saw him forget those two vital things again. I was quietly proud of Andrew. He had remembered what I had told him about how he could be a big help to Alex as long as he always kept in mind that, while he might know more about running *Visitor IV* than Alex did at first, Alex was still the boss. Tact was not something you could teach anyone. I had seen little of it among my West Indian crewmen over the years, but Andrew was an exceptional young man. I wish I had had him in the beginning.

After the power and telephone lines were taken off and secured in their places on the dock, Alex again asked Andrew to take in the lines. Andrew went to work on them in the proper sequence I had taught him. As the last line was set on the dock, Alex reached for the shifts. I could see his hands were trembling.

"Wait a minute," I said.

Alex stopped and looked at me. "What for?" he asked, breathlessly.

"Is your mouth dry?" I asked him.

"You damn betcha!" he replied with a grin.

"Good," I said. "I just wanted to make sure you were having all the right reactions. Incidentally, notice the boat. We are still alongside the dock. There is very rarely any wind here and never any current. Also, it takes a lot to get this 41-ton boat in motion. It isn't like a little boat where, the minute you let your lines go, you have to do something with the engines. She might sit here for two or three minutes without moving any appreciable amount. My point is, take your time. The boat is in no hurry and won't be, unless you rush it. OK, back her out."

And so it went, for another two days. I reviewed everything I knew about boat handling, especially twin-engine work, which was completely new to Alex. Alex did very well. Nervous, yes, but so was I and so would anyone else be, the first time they took out a boat more than twice the size of anything they had handled before. Oddly enough, a bigger boat is easier to dock than a little one. They have a tendency to behave better and to be responsive to what they are told. Of course, there are a lot of places you don't want to get into with a big boat, or you will be in big trouble, fast. But, if you have the room to move about, you can do anything with a big boat that you can do with a small one, and you can probably do it more easily.

I think Alex was as exhausted as I was, by the time he left. We had put in an intensive week. About a month or so later, Alex's son, Bo, as he was called, came down for a week and I checked him out on the operation, as well. Evidently, Bo would be running *Visitor* during his summer vacations from college, and Alex would come down for the rest of the months, until he was ready to retire completely.

That last season was a busy one for me. I was chartering and, at the same time, packing up and making arrangements to leave. There were also some last minute little jobs to be done on *Visitor*, which I felt I owed her, if not Alex.

Packing was a drag. Despite all the moving around I have done in my life, I have never been able to be blasé about leaving a place and friends I had come to love. There was real sadness in throwing out things I had saved over the years, thinking there might be a use for them. Now they had to go, because I knew they would not be used. Old papers had to be gone through and weeded out. Clothes that I knew I wouldn't use again had to go.

Going through *Visitor*'s nooks and crannies, looking for my personal things to pack, I began to feel as though she were watching me. I felt like a traitor, or a thief working in the night. Melodramatic? Maybe. But that's the way I felt, just the same. It was as though I were turning my back on someone who had treated me well, someone whom I had loved. Of course it was stupid. *Visitor* was nothing but a block of wood with an iron heart.

But Sam knew. Beverly had brought Sam to me two years ago, hidden in her pocket. He was a tiny Siamese kitten, just

192

weaned from his mother, who was Beverly's pet. Sam knew that I was leaving. He decided not to wait until the last. Two weeks before I left St. Lucia, Sam disappeared from the boat and I never saw him again.

Finally, I had reduced the things I was taking with me on the plane to one large suitcase. Everything that was to go sea freight was turned over to the shipping company. In true West Indian fashion, the company lost track of my things for two months, so I didn't receive them until four months later. Alex arrived in St. Lucia two days before I was to leave and we did a lot of last minute talking about *Visitor* and the business.

There was a final charter the day before my flight. I asked Alex if he would mind if I were to go along simply as a passenger. I had always wondered what it would be like to go for a day charter on *Visitor IV* and have rum punch brought to me while I sat on the bow, not worrying about a damn thing. Of course, Alex agreed to my plan. I tried hard not to tighten up in my stomach when he backed *Visitor* out of her slip and when he brought her alongside the treacherous jetty at Soufriere, but it wasn't easy. My little friends at the jetty couldn't understand why "Visitor Four", as they had come to call me, was sitting on the bow, rather than standing in the wheelhouse.

I sat with Mrs. Allain in her kitchen and did my best to thank her for all the wonderful food she had given my charterers over the past three years, but that wasn't easy either. She and I lived in two different worlds, but we had become good friends in the best way we knew how. I don't think it was easy for either of us to say good-by. There was a lot of talk about my coming back some day to say hello, and that helped. It was the first time that I didn't feel like eating her lunch. She insisted on putting some Creole chicken in a bag for me. What a wonderful, dear lady she was.

My little friends at the jetty were full of fun, as usual, and I threw the last of my St. Lucian coins into the water for them to dive after.

"Hey! Visitor Four! Small change! I dive it up like a shark!"

193

they shouted. They ran off the edge of the jetty and splashed into the water, scooping up the coins and popping to the surface with wet, beaming faces.

I had my last look at my favorite sight on St. Lucia, Anse des Pitons. I tried to soak up its island beauty, so that I could remember it always. We made our usual stop for swimming at Anse Chastenet. I donned my swimsuit and face mask and had my last look at the coral, the sponges and all the tropical fish. I even swam down to check for wear on the mooring chain and line, to make sure it would continue to serve Alex as well as it had me. When I came out of the water, Andrew was there at the top of the swimming ladder with a rum punch for me. What a fine crewman he was!

We made the slow cruise through Marigot Bay, which was always a pleasant spot, but I still preferred Anse des Pitons. Coming toward Vigie Creek, Alex did a fine job of threading his way through the yachts in the anchorage. I remember thinking that he would probably do all right with *Visitor*, despite his lack of experience. He made a good docking, Andrew snapped to the lines like the pro that he was, then Alex turned off the engines. I heard them stop for the last time.

That cruise was something I had always wanted to do. I had thought about it and planned it for years. I knew I would do it when *Visitor* was sold, even if I had to pay my way. And I'm glad that I did go. But it was one of the saddest days of my life.

The next morning, my plane was to leave at ten o'clock, which left me too much time. I didn't like that all. I said good-by to Andrew when he came to work and gave him the letter of recommendation I had promised him. If things didn't work out well with Alex, he would need it when he went job-hunting. I found Beverly in her office. She looked about the same as she had when we had met three years ago: a trim little blond in a tiny, bright-colored bikini and a cover-up, and she was still full of sass.

"So we're finally getting rid of you, are we?" she asked with a smile.

"You are," I said. "Who'll you have to bitch at when I'm

194

gone?"

We exchanged a few more pleasantries and a jibe or two, just to keep in practice, then I was out of her office with the door closed behind me. A lot of things had happened to me since I had first opened that door and I wouldn't have traded any one of them for anything in the world.

I walked down the cement breakwater toward *Visitor* to pick up my bag. I had my eye out for George; I knew he was working on one of the nearby boats. I found him, went up to him and had to call his name to get him to look up. George saw me and looked embarrassed. I think George and I were good friends too, in our own ways. I had a lot of respect for him as a craftsman doing the best he could with what he had, and I respected him for his pride and honesty, as well. We had never talked about anything personal and I had no idea what George really thought of me, but I would like to think that if I had one St. Lucian friend, one St. Lucian who really would be glad to see me again, it would be George.

"You leavin, Mr. Bob?" George asked.

"Yes, George." It was all I could say.

We shook hands and I had to turn and head for *Visitor*. There were a lot of things I would like to have said to George, but I couldn't. There had been too many good-bys that morning and too many good memories were crowding into my head. I was filled with sadness.

I stepped aboard *Visitor* for the last time and picked up my bag. Alex offered to drive me to the airport, but I declined. I said I had walked to *Visitor* from the airport with my bag in hand three years ago and I was just enough of a sentimental slob to want to leave the same way. I said it in an offhand way, but I meant every word of it. We shook hands and wished each other good luck. I stepped off *Visitor* onto the dock and headed up the dirt road toward the airport. I knew just where I could stop for a moment to take a last look at *Visitor*. She looked a damn sight better boat than she had the first time I had seen her, and I *knew* she *was* a damn sight better boat than when I had first seen her. Maybe that's all there was to it.

195

EPILOGUE

I had been back in the United States about six months and was settled into another public relations job at a small advertising agency, when I received a postcard from a person in St. Lucia to whom I had recently written. It said:

Dear Bob,
Good to hear from you. Glad all's well. Will write details later but just to let you know Alex Harkness ran *Visitor IV* over the Soufriere reef and wrecked it on Anse Chastenet beach. Just odd bits of wood to show for that lovely boat.

All for now,